NATURAL RESOURCES IN LATIN AMERICA AND THE CARIBBEAN

BEYOND BOOMS AND BUSTS?

NATURAL RESOURCES IN LATIN AMERICA AND THE CARIBBEAN

BEYOND BOOMS AND BUSTS?

Emily Sinnott
John Nash
Augusto de la Torre

THE WORLD BANK
Washington, D.C.

© 2010 The International Bank for Reconstruction and Development/The World Bank
1818 H Street, NW
Washington, DC 20433
Telephone: 202-473-1000
Internet: www.worldbank.org

1 2 3 4 13 12 11 10

This volume is a product of the staff of the International Bank for Reconstruction and Development/The World Bank. The findings, interpretations, and conclusions expressed in this volume do not necessarily reflect the views of the Executive Directors of The World Bank or the governments they represent.

The World Bank does not guarantee the accuracy of the data included in this work. The boundaries, colors, denominations, and other information shown on any map in this work do not imply any judgement on the part of The World Bank concerning the legal status of any territory or the endorsement or acceptance of such boundaries.

ISBN: 978-0-8213-8482-4
eISBN: 978-0-8213-8492-3
DOI: 10.1596/978-0-8213-8482-4

Library of Congress Cataloging-in-Publication Data
Torre, Augusto de la.
  Natural resources in Latin America and the Caribbean : beyond booms and busts? / Augusto de la Torre, Emily Sinnott, John Nash.
    p. cm.
  Includes bibliographical references and index.
  ISBN 978-0-8213-8482-4 — ISBN 978-0-8213-8492-3 (electronic)
  1. Natural resources—Latin America. 2. Natural resources—Caribbean Area. I. Sinnott, Emily. II. Nash, John, 1953- III. Title.
  HC85.T67 2010
  333.7098—dc22
                                                                                    2010022086

Cover design: Naylor Design, Inc.

Contents

Acknowledgments

Natural Resources in Latin America and the Caribbean: Beyond Booms and Busts? summarizes the output of a large research project on commodities that the Latin America and the Caribbean Region of the World Bank has embarked upon over the past year. The report is truly a collective effort, having been built on a sizeable collection of background papers by economists and political scientists within and outside the World Bank. We are very grateful to the authors of the background papers for their contributions. We regret that certain papers have been overused and others underused given the wealth of background material they contain. It is our hope that this body of work will continue to assist researchers in the field in future years.

The report was prepared by three units of the Latin American and the Caribbean Region of the World Bank: the Office of the Chief Economist, the Poverty Reduction and Management Department, and the Sustainable Development Department. It was prepared by a core team led by Emily Sinnott and John Nash, and consisting of Barbara Cunha, Ole Hagen Jorgensen, Glenn Morgan, and Carlos Prada Lombo, under the overall direction of Augusto de la Torre. The team benefited from the guidance and advice of Marcelo Giugale and Laura Tuck.

We particularly thank our reviewers, Phil Keefer, (World Bank), Bill Maloney (World Bank), and John Tilton (Colorado School of Mines), for their very careful reading of early versions of the report and their extensive and constructive suggestions, which contributed to shaping our own thinking on many issues. The team gained much also from the input of participants in the background authors' workshops held in Washington, D.C., in September and October 2009.

Background papers were prepared by Richard Auty (Lancaster University), Juan Carlos Beluasteguigoitia (World Bank), Mauro Boianovsky (University of Brasilia), Irene Brambilla (Yale University), Joseph Byrne (University of Glasgow), Oscar Calvo-Gonzalez (World Bank), Máximo Camacho (University of Murcia), Roberto Chang (Rutgers University), Simón Cueva (University of the Americas, Ecuador), John Dick (consultant, World Bank), Thad Dunning (Yale University), Eduardo Engel (Yale University), Giorgio Fazio (University of Glasgow), Norbert Fiess (World Bank), Jeffrey Frankel (Harvard University), Constantino Hevia (World Bank), Miguel Kiguel (EconViews, Buenos Aires), Daniel Lederman (World Bank), Daniella Llanos (Harvard University), Norman Loayza (World Bank), Benjamin Mandel (Federal Reserve Board of Governors), Patricio Navia (New York University),

Christopher Neilson (Yale University), Javier Okseniuk (University of Buenos Aires), Gabriel Pérez (Bank of Spain), Guido Porto (University of La Plata), Justin Ram (London School of Economics), Marcelo Regúnaga (University of Buenos Aires), Michael Ross (UCLA), Giovanni Ruta (World Bank), Rashmi Shankar (World Bank), Carlos Toranzo (Latin American Institute of Social Research, La Paz), Riccardo Trezzi (World Bank), Rodrigo Valdes (IMF), Felix Várdy (University of California at Berkeley and IMF), Steven Webb (World Bank), and Colin Xu (World Bank).

The report benefited from specific contributions or comments by John Baffes (World Bank), Erik Bloom (World Bank), César Calderón (World Bank), Ashley Camhi (World Bank), Mauricio Cárdenas (Brookings Institution), Diego Cerdeiro (World Bank), Rodrigo Chaves (World Bank), Edith Cortes (World Bank), Adriana de la Huerta (University of Chicago), Alberto Díaz-Cayeros (University of California, San Diego), Louise Cord (World Bank), Tito Cordella (World Bank), Francisco Ferreira (World Bank), Christian Gonzalez (World Bank), Stephen Haber (Stanford University), Alain Ize (World Bank), Carlos Felipe Jaramillo (World Bank), Kai Kaiser (World Bank), Kieran Kelleher (World Bank), Steve Knack (World Bank), Stefan Koeberle (World Bank), Donald Larson (World Bank), Eduardo Ley (World Bank), Julio Loayza (World Bank), Nick Manning (World Bank), William Magrath (World Bank), Anil Markandya (World Bank), Victor Menaldo (University of Washington), Carlos Muñoz (Instituto Nacional de Ecología, Mexico), Rolando Ossowski (Independent Public Policy Professional), Stefano Pagiola (World Bank), Chris Papageorgiou (IMF), Guillermo Perry (Fedesarrollo, Bogota, and Center for Global Development), Roberto Rigobón (MIT), Jamele Rigolini (World Bank), Maurice Schiff (World Bank), Luis Servén (World Bank), Julio Velasco (World Bank), Lorena Vinuela (World Bank), Deborah Wetzel (World Bank), and Alonso Zarzar (World Bank).

Erika Bazan Lavanda, Ruth Delgado, and Tammy Lynn Pertillar provided excellent editorial and production support for the report.

Finally, we appreciate the assistance provided by Santiago Pombo Bejarano, Patricia Katayama, Andrès Meneses, and Dina Towbin in the World Bank's Office of the Publisher on the report's publication and dissemination activities.

Foreword

Throughout the history of the Latin America and Caribbean (LAC) region, natural resource wealth has been critical for its economies. Production of precious metals, sugar, rubber, grains, coffee, copper, and oil have at various periods of history made countries in Latin America—and their colonial powers—some of the most prosperous in the world. In some ways, these commodities may have changed the course of history in the world at large. Latin America produced around 80 percent of the world's silver in the 16th through 19th centuries, fueling the monetary systems of not only Europe, but China and India as well. And because so much of the riches brought to Brazil by the discovery of gold in the late 1600s were spent on imports from England, some historians argue that this was instrumental in laying the foundation for the Industrial Revolution. Although LAC is now a relatively urbanized and industrialized region among developing countries, commodity production and exports continue to be key for countries that account for a very large part of the population and share of economic activity in the region.

Yet the fact that LAC, with all its natural riches, has failed to grow in parallel with countries that have now achieved high-income status raises the question, "Have resources been more of a curse than a blessing for the region?" Certainly, the recurrent patterns of commodity price booms and busts have created significant uncertainty for LAC, net exporters and net importers alike. Yet a number of the countries that are now high income have been highly commodity dependent but seemed to use this wealth as a springboard for development. And today, among countries in LAC and other developing regions, some appear to be managing these cycles better than others. It would seem that there is much that can be learned from these experiences and from the large body of economic research on the subject.

The dramatic movements in commodity markets since the early 2000s, as well as the recent economic crisis, provide new data to analyze and also underscore the importance of a better understanding of issues related to boom-bust commodity cycles. The current pattern of global recovery has favored LAC so far. Countercyclical policies have supported domestic demand in the larger LAC economies, and external demand from fast-growing emerging markets has boosted exports and terms of trade for LAC's net commodity exporters. Prospects for LAC in the short term look good.

Beyond the cyclical rebound, however, the region's major longer-run challenge going forward will be to craft a bold productivity agenda. With LAC coming out of this crisis relatively well positioned, this may well be possible, especially considering that the region's improved macro-financial resiliency gives greater assurance that future gains from growth will not be wiped out by financial crises. In addition, LAC has been making significant strides in the equity agenda and this could help mobilize consensus in favor of a long overdue growth-oriented reform agenda. But it remains to be seen whether the region will be able to seize the opportunity to boost long-run growth, especially considering the large gaps that LAC would need to close in such key areas as saving, human capital accumulation, physical infrastructure, and the ability to adopt and adapt new technologies.

LAC's natural resource wealth can help seize the growth opportunity both by providing governments with greater fiscal space and by serving directly as a key source of growth if properly managed. But this opportunity will only be realized if windfall earnings are managed judiciously within a long-term horizon, so as to avoid falling victim to the "natural resource curse," as has sometimes happened in past cycles. The downside risks of commodity abundance can be avoided, if commodity-exporting countries manage to save (via cyclically adjusted primary fiscal surpluses) a substantial fraction of the commodity-related revenue windfalls.

In that context, this year's regional flagship study follows in the footsteps of several other reports from the Latin America and the Caribbean Chief Economist's Office on various aspects of commodity dependence. I believe that the time is right for a more in-depth examination. I hope that the new analysis and research conducted as part of this study will advance the frontiers of knowledge and prove to be of practical value in helping countries take full advantage of the opportunities presented by their natural resources.

Pamela Cox
Vice President, Latin America & the Caribbean
The World Bank

Abbreviations

BB	balanced budget		IT	information technology
CARE	Cooperation for American Relief Everywhere		LAC	Latin America and the Caribbean
			LIBOR	London Interbank Offered Rate
CERC	Centro de Estudios de la Realidad Contemporánea (Center for the Study of Contemporary Reality)		LPG	liquefied petroleum gas
			MUV	manufactures unit value index
			OECD	Organisation for Economic Co-operation and Development
CMI	Ministerial Committee for Innovation			
CNIC	National Innovation Council for Competitiveness		OLADE	Organización Latinoamericana de Energia (Latin America Energy Organization)
CPI	consumer price index		OPEC	Organization of Petroleum Exporting Countries
DRP	Doe Run Peru			
EITI	Extractive Industries Transparency Initiative		PAMA	Programa de Adecuación y Manejo Ambiental (Environmental Remediation and Management Program)
FEM	Fondo de Estabilización Macroeconómica			
FIC	Competitiveness and Innovation Fund			
GDP	gross domestic product		PEP	peg the export price
GNI	gross national income		PES	payment for environmental services
IBRD	International Bank for Reconstruction and Development		PPI	producer price index
			SOTE	Trans-Ecuadorian Oil Pipeline System
IMF	International Monetary Fund		UN	United Nations
INE	Instituto Nacional de Ecología		WWF	World Wildlife Fund

CHAPTER 1

Introduction

The mural of the economic history of Latin America and the Caribbean (LAC) has been painted in the colors of its commodities: the gold and silver that attracted early explorers and conquistadores, the "green gold" of sugar, the rich brown of coffee, the magenta of cochineal, copper, and the "black gold" in the 20th century, to name just a few. Commodity exports have always powered the economies of the region, filled its governments' coffers, and served as its main link to global markets. These exports have in some periods played an important role in shaping the economies of other regions of the world. Yet the apparent conundrum that, with all of their natural riches, many countries in LAC have lagged in development has attracted the attention and comment of economists since the beginning of the profession.

This situation led some to conclude that something inherent in commodity production must be prejudicial to an economy's prospects for growth. Adam Smith asserted in *The Wealth of Nations* that mining was the industry that "a prudent law-giver, who desired to increase the capital of his nation, would least choose to give any extraordinary encouragement." The question of how to treat commodity production continues to bedevil "prudent lawgivers" in modern times, particularly in the wake of recent volatility in global markets. Managing these recurrent cycles of booms and busts has always challenged policy makers in commodity-dependent countries. In the LAC region, where commodity production has always played such a vital economic role, it is at or near the top of the policy agenda. The objective of this report is to provide support to policy makers who have to deal with the many associated issues.

Despite the many examples of commodity-rich countries that are lagging in development, a consensus has yet to emerge on the impact of natural resources on economic growth. For each example of a "cursed" country, another can be found of a country rich in natural resources that managed its resources well and achieved high growth. And recent evidence suggests that, overall, natural resources may indeed have a positive impact on growth. The upside of commodity dependence has been underscored in the recent financial crisis. Even with the subprime crisis spreading through the industrial world, LAC economies remained effectively "de-coupled" from August 2007 until mid-2008, with growth continuing as long as commodity prices remained high. Worldwide, the countries suffering the worst growth collapses in the recession were those with higher shares of manufacturing exports. And now in the recovery, LAC is making a fairly strong rebound, buoyed by demand for commodity exports in China and other emerging markets. Looking forward, LAC may derive significant benefits from being the mine and granary for those economies.

The fact that abundant natural resources do not necessarily hinder growth does not imply, however, that they inevitably lead to growth. Variance across countries remains high, and many examples show that a curse can emerge if resources are poorly managed. In recent years, economists have posited and investigated channels for commodity production to have adverse effects on a country's economic welfare and institutions—or on medium- and long-term growth prospects.

In this report, we look at the evidence on the "big picture" of the commodity curse, but much of the report is focused on examining more specific channels, which might be called "commodity concerns." We broadly group these concerns into four sets. One deals with the direct economic effects of commodity dependence and the implications for long-term growth (chapter 3). Another deals with the interactions between commodity production and the rents it generates, on one hand, and a country's institutions on the other (chapter 4). A third deals with the macroeconomic challenges of managing the volatility of revenue flows, including the distributional implications at the household level posed by cyclical social spending (chapter 5). And a fourth set is associated with potential negative environmental and social impacts (chapter 6). Chapter 7 explores the policy implications of the analysis of the preceding chapters. Before entering this issues-oriented discussion, however, in chapter 2 we lay out the salient stylized facts of commodity production and trade in LAC. In this introduction, we briefly discuss the features of commodities that make them special and the associated implications for the issues explored in the rest of the report.

What Makes Commodities Different, and Why Does It Matter?

For this study, commodities are defined as traded, nonbranded, bulk goods with little processing—their quality and characteristics can be objectively established, and they are supplied without qualitative differentiation across a market. Under our definition, then, commodities are natural resources (minerals, oil, and gas) or goods produced directly by exploiting natural resources (as in agriculture). So, we use these terms interchangeably.

Several characteristics of commodities distinguish them from other kinds of products or economic activities, leading to different economic, political, and social effects in countries dependent on their production or sale. Some of these characteristics are common across all commodities; others are more pronounced in hydro-carbon and mineral industries than in agricultural product markets. Among the specifics that commodities are commonly considered to have, the most important for the questions investigated in this report are explored below:

- *Commodity sectors—especially minerals and hydrocarbons—produce high rents.* In countries with abundant natural resources that are easily produced at low cost, the extraction and sale of these resources in world markets generates large rents—that is, profits above normal returns on investments.[1] Even in countries where high fixed costs hold down long-run returns, resource extraction tends to generate high cash flows—sometimes called quasi rents—following the initial investment, because variable (operating) costs are typically low.

High rents generate two potential dangers. The first is a pure economic effect: high rents during a period of commodity export bonanza tend to cause the real exchange rate to appreciate and to attract resources from other activities, discouraging diversification of noncommodity exports: the Dutch disease. Specializing in commodity production would not be perceived as a problem were it not for two other allegations, which are contentious but have nevertheless been influential in the debate over the years. One is the famous Prebisch-Singer hypothesis that postulates that international commodity prices have followed a declining secular trend, implying that countries relying mainly on commodity exports will suffer from declining terms of trade. This was an important intellectual underpinning for the industry-led, import-substitution growth strategies adopted by many countries in the region during the 1950s–1970s. A second is the idea that natural resource exploitation has low potential for linkages, product upgrading, and economic spillovers in other sectors.

The second danger of rents, which we deem quite important for LAC and to which we devote an entire chapter, is institutional. This pool of easy money, especially when combined with government ownership, creates conditions conducive to rent seeking and poor governance, and can undermine the development of good institutions and, consequently, of long-term growth. Although low-cost agricultural production does generate substantial rents at times—as seen, for example, in coffee in Colombia, Brazil, and Central America during past booms, and more recently in oilseeds and grains in Brazil and the Southern Cone—these are generally ephemeral and hard for governments to capture. As a result, they do not often generate the same degree of fiscal problems and rentier effects associated with exhaustible resources. Dutch disease effects may, however, be significant for these commodities as well.

• *International commodity prices are highly volatile because of relatively inelastic supply and demand.* This is true at least in the short term. Fluctuations of price indexes for each of the major commodity groups are much higher than those of, say, manufacturing unit value indexes (see figure 3.5). Terms-of-trade volatility is highest for fuel exporting countries, followed by other commodity exporters and then by countries that specialize in manufacturing exports (see, for example, Baxter and Koupartisas 2006). Price volatility increases uncertainty and risk in the entire economy, which may discourage investment. Combined with real exchange rate appreciations during commodity booms, it may also foster concentrated export baskets, which can in turn heighten the adverse effects of price volatility on the economy. In conjunction with high fiscal dependence from commodity revenues, it also leads to instability in government revenues and difficulties in macroeconomic management. For households, price volatility has different effects depending on whether income (or expenditure) depends significantly on commodity production (or consumption). But if a price shock creates a need for higher social spending just as it lowers the government's revenues, managing public expenditures becomes difficult. Price cycles can also create a political dynamic that leads to governance problems in the commodity sectors, such as repeated cycles of privatization and nationalization.

• *Exploitation of mineral and hydrocarbon resources requires high initial investment with long and uncertain time horizons for payback, creating disincentives for private investment.* Large upfront sunk costs are required for oil exploration and drilling, pipeline construction, and mine excavation. Technological advances have made exploration much less uncertain, but production remains technically risky, and policy risks, such as price controls and nationalization, remain relevant. Such investment disincentives can be overcome through a favorable business environment, as many examples of extensive private investment show. But often, risks and sunk costs have led to government domination of production and sometimes to poor governance and excessive fiscal reliance on natural resource revenues.

• *Mineral and hydrocarbon resources are not renewable.* Although new discoveries, technological advances, and price movements can increase proven reserves, the stock of mineral and hydrocarbon resources is fixed. (In contrast, agricultural, forestry, and fishery resources can regenerate, if slowly, for forests and fisheries.) To generate a sustainable growth path that optimally benefits current and future generations, natural wealth must be transformed into other forms of capital. This has been a considerable policy challenge, particularly where appropriate institutions are absent.

• *The natural resource may be common property and the exploitation technology may produce negative externalities.* Some resources (fisheries, pools of oil and gas, publicly owned forests) are quintessential common property: they are relatively nonexclusionary (once discovered, it is costly to exclude others from using them) and "subtractable" (if one person uses some of the resource, less is available for others). Without public or private mechanisms to regulate their use, the frequent result is overexploitation: the tragedy of the commons. Moreover, even where it may be fairly easy to prevent others from extracting resources—minerals, say—extraction generates wastes that require disposal, often imposing costs on others by polluting water, soil, or air, effectively using environmental services as a public good and creating large negative externalities. These external costs are often borne by local populations, especially indigenous peoples, who are least capable of dealing with them, and such situations have at times fomented social conflict.

- *Exploitation often takes place through enclave production in specific locations.* Commodity production is, by nature, immobile: it must take place where the resources are. Even for agricultural commodities, for which the appropriate area is larger than for minerals and hydrocarbons, limits are imposed by climate, soil type, infrastructure, and other constraints, so production tends to be geographically concentrated. This often creates tensions—and sometimes armed conflicts—over resource ownership and the associated rents, as local inhabitants or local governments challenge the central government's claims. It also limits the options for mitigating environmental damage through appropriate site selection, because the optimal areas for exploitation may be environmentally sensitive.

These factors specific to commodity production interact in dynamic ways, and they can affect economic growth, institutions, and social stability through a number of channels. Many of the complexities in resource management are created by the intertemporal nature of the decisions and policy actions required to deal with these interactions.

A recurring theme in this report is that commodity price volatility and the rents associated with resource extraction can together generate vicious cycles, affecting economic structures and governance institutions. The price shocks tend to cause large fluctuations in the real exchange rate, which discourage diversification, leading to concentration of the production and export structures and of the government's revenue base. This concentration then increases the share of economic activity and fiscal revenues exposed to price shocks—the "value at risk" in the terminology of financial risk management—making the economy and the government's fiscal position even more vulnerable to future shocks. Responding to this requires that the government engage in active anticyclical expenditure policies across short-term price cycles, as well as save some of the resource wealth over long time periods. This behavior is politically difficult to sustain unless the electorate trusts the government to manage the savings wisely. Yet the pool of rents can have a corrosive effect on governance structures, undermining the very trust needed to allow the government to credibly make such a commitment. After describing in chapter 2 some facts about commodity markets that are relevant for the rest of the report, we explore these interactions in the succeeding chapters.

Endnote

1. The natural resource economics literature draws a distinction between Ricardian rents and Hotelling rents. For purposes of the issues considered in this report, the distinction is not very relevant, and we note here only that the rents accruing to mineral and hydrocarbon producers have elements of both.

CHAPTER 2

Stylized Facts of Commodity Production and Trade in LAC

Natural resource production shows considerable heterogeneity across LAC countries along a number of dimensions. Before analyzing the implications of natural resources for long-term growth and development, we look at what unites and divides LAC countries in their resource exploitation and management, benchmarking these factors with other commodity exporters in the world. We summarize the most important similarities and differences in seven stylized facts.

Fact 1: Commodity exports are important for most of the region, as measured by economic size, population, or geographical area. The more populous and economically larger countries in the region—Mexico and the South American nations—tend to be net commodity exporters. The less populous and smaller countries—mostly in Central America and the Caribbean—tend to be net commodity importers. Net commodity exporters house 93 percent of the LAC population and contribute 97 percent to LAC GDP (figure 2.1). In numbers, however, they make up just more than half of the LAC countries. The net commodity importers are mainly in Central America and the Caribbean. A country's status as an exporter or importer determines whether it gains or loses when commodity prices move sharply up or down. Thus, while most of the larger economies were substantial winners from the 2001–08 commodity boom, smaller countries in Central America and the Caribbean did lose. Using a net commodity trade price

index (the weighted ratio of the commodity exports and commodity imports price index), the biggest losers were El Salvador (–39 percent) and Guatemala (–34 percent), while the biggest winners were Bolivia (261 percent) and República Bolivariana de Venezuela (149 percent).[1] The seven largest economies on average gained 22 percent. Of course, it is worth keeping in mind that, especially in a heavily urbanized region such as LAC, a large part of the population, especially the poor, are losers when prices of essential or socially sensitive commodities (such as foods and fuels) rise.

Fact 2: Compared with high-income resource-abundant countries, LAC commodity exporters have much lower (known) natural resource endowments per capita but are much more dependent on natural resource revenues. This lack of diversification of revenue sources creates challenges, which we discuss further below. Perhaps surprisingly, when expressed in per capita terms, natural resource abundance in Latin America remains significantly lower than in high-income, commodity-rich exporter countries (figure 2.2). Note, however, that abundance—if equated to a country's proven reserves—is not fixed over time. As Wright (1990) argues, resource abundance mainly reflects "greater exploitation of geological potential." Institutions and innovation policies affect not only how a country uses its natural resources but also whether it exploits natural riches in the first place. David and Wright (1997) identify an accommodating legal environment,

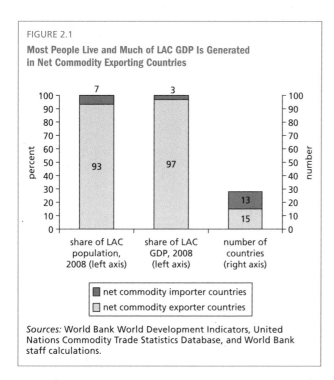

FIGURE 2.1

Most People Live and Much of LAC GDP Is Generated in Net Commodity Exporting Countries

Sources: World Bank World Development Indicators, United Nations Commodity Trade Statistics Database, and World Bank staff calculations.

investment in public knowledge, and education in mining and metallurgy as factors that made possible the rapid exploration and exploitation of mineral deposits in the United States. One explanation put forward for the late exploitation of resources in Latin America is the "lack of accurate knowledge about the extent and distribution of mineral deposits" (Wright 2001).

Even so, LAC commodity exporters rely much more on fiscal revenues from commodity production: despite having a similar GDP share of fiscal revenues from commodity production (around 6 versus 5 percent for advanced resource-rich producers), LAC producers derive on average 24 percent of total fiscal revenues from commodities compared with 9 percent for the advanced resource-rich economies (figure 2.3). Much of LAC's GDP is also generated in countries that rely heavily on fiscal revenues from commodity production. Of the seven economies (LAC-7), which make up

FIGURE 2.2

Abundance in LAC Is Modest Relative to High-Income Resource-Rich Countries

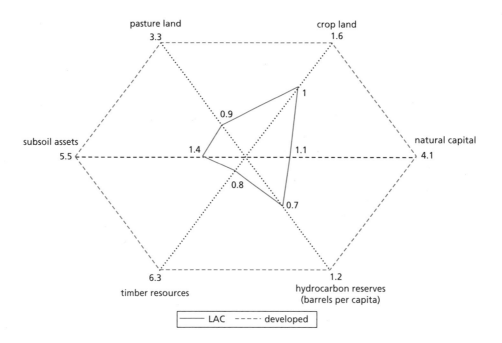

Sources: World Bank Natural Capital Database (World Bank 2006), British Petroleum Statistical Yearbook 2009, and World Bank staff calculations.
Note: Capital variables are equal to [sum (capital of each country (in levels)) / sum (population of each country)] / [capital world / population world]. For all variables, with the exception of hydrocarbon reserves, LAC corresponds to LAC-7 countries plus Bolivia, Ecuador, and Trinidad and Tobago. For hydrocarbon reserves, Chile is excluded. Developed countries include Australia, Canada, New Zealand, and Norway for natural capital variables. New Zealand is excluded from the hydrocarbon reserves category. Values for natural capital variables are for 2000; those for hydrocarbon proven reserves are for 2008.

FIGURE 2.3

LAC Is, However, More Dependent on Commodities, Especially Fiscally

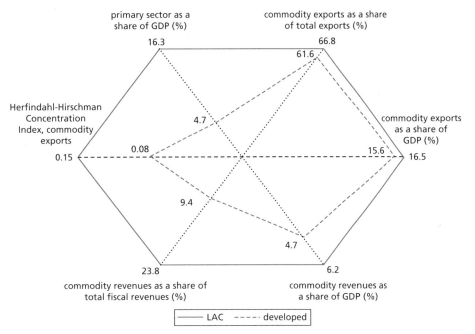

Sources: World Bank World Development Indicators, UN Commodity Trade Statistics Database, national authorities, IMF, and World Bank staff calculations.
Note: For the fiscal variables, the groups use the hydrocarbon and mineral producers only, because revenue from production of other commodities is typically not reported separately from other revenue sources. Thus the countries for each group were Bolivia, Chile, Colombia, Ecuador, Peru, Trinidad and Tobago, and República Bolivariana de Venezuela for LAC, and Canada and Norway for the high-income category. For the remaining variables, we used the LAC-7 countries plus Bolivia, Ecuador, and Trinidad and Tobago for LAC, and Australia, Canada, Norway, and New Zealand for the high-income category. These were the countries in each group that ranked in the top 50 among worldwide commodity exporters (as a share of their total exports) and had a population of more than half a million people.

approximately 85 percent of regional GDP, six have a substantial commodity revenue share in overall revenues, ranging from 10 to 49 percent on average over 2004–08. The six are Argentina (agricultural export commodities), Chile (copper), Colombia (oil), Mexico (hydrocarbons), Peru (mining), and República Bolivariana de Venezuela (hydrocarbons). Oil revenues in the remaining LAC-7 economy, Brazil, are also growing with recent discoveries. In addition to the LAC-7 countries, some smaller economies in the region are highly dependent on commodity revenues, particularly the hydrocarbon producers Bolivia (natural gas), Ecuador (petroleum), and Trinidad and Tobago (hydrocarbons).

The share of natural resources in total revenues has increased in the last decade in all LAC commodity-exporting countries except Mexico (figure 2.4). The increase has been largely fueled by higher prices in both oil and non-oil commodities, although higher production has also contributed, as have increased tax rates on

minerals in Chile, Peru, and Bolivia. For many countries, the growing dependence on commodities as a source of fiscal revenue has been matched by an increase in dependence on commodity revenues to finance large increases in fiscal spending. Chile is a notable exception: while its public spending did increase every year from 1999 to 2009, it saved a large share of the copper boom.

Fact 3: The share of natural resources in overall exports has declined over time, but much less so than in some other emerging regions, and it remains relatively large. So, LAC remains more vulnerable to terms-of-trade shocks than it would be with a more diversified export basket. Since the 1970s, the share of commodities in exports has fallen all over the world. But the importance of commodities in LAC's export basket has declined far less than in other middle-income regions such as East Asia, South Asia, and Eastern Europe and Central Asia (figure 2.5). Commodities still account for half the value of total exports.

FIGURE 2.4

Fiscal Revenues from Natural Resources Have Grown in Importance for Many LAC Commodity Exporters

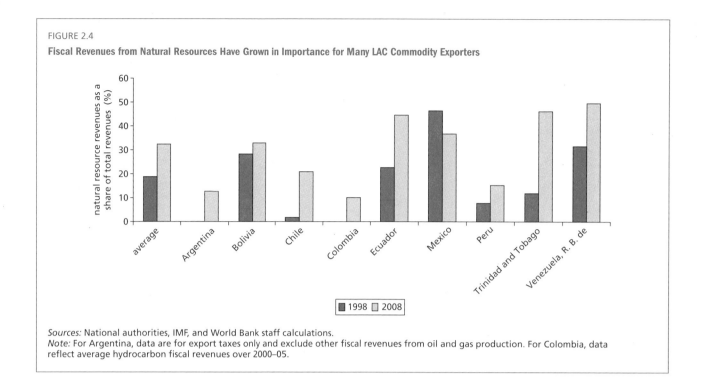

Sources: National authorities, IMF, and World Bank staff calculations.
Note: For Argentina, data are for export taxes only and exclude other fiscal revenues from oil and gas production. For Colombia, data reflect average hydrocarbon fiscal revenues over 2000–05.

FIGURE 2.5

The Decline in the Share of Commodity Exports Has Been Lower for LAC, the Middle East, and Africa

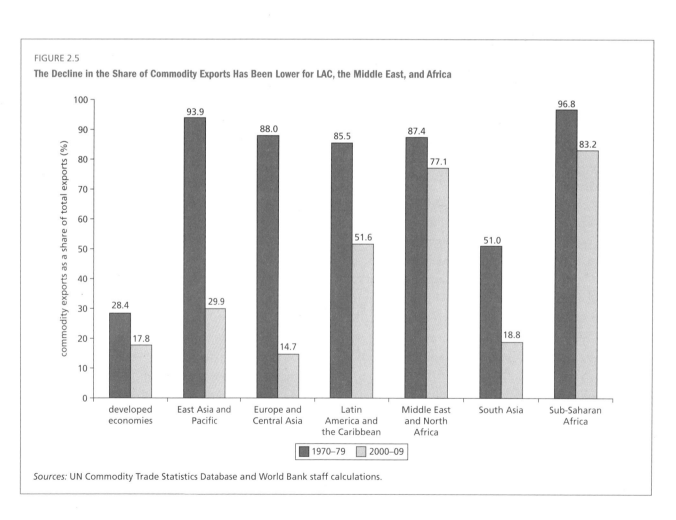

Sources: UN Commodity Trade Statistics Database and World Bank staff calculations.

Although this remains significantly lower than in the Middle East or Sub-Saharan Africa, it shows that Latin America has managed to diversify exports significantly less than East Asia or Eastern Europe and Central Asia, where in 30 years the commodity share in exports was reduced from around 90 percent to 30 percent or even 15 percent.

There has, however, been great heterogeneity among LAC countries, with dependence remaining high for some countries (Chile, Peru, and República Bolivariana de Venezuela continue to have a commodity share of more than 75 percent of exports) and falling much more dramatically for others (such as Brazil and Mexico). There have also been significant changes in composition in many countries. Except for copper in Chile and oil in Colombia and República Bolivariana de Venezuela, the top two commodity exports in 2006 are different in all of the LAC-7 countries from the top products in 1962. And although commodity exports lost importance in the merchandise basket in LAC, they still expanded in absolute value over time.

Fact 4: Since the 1990s, LAC commodity exports have become more concentrated in value terms around fewer commodities, while the increasing concentration in destination markets over the early 1980s to mid-1990s has reversed somewhat. The product concentration of LAC commodity exports (in value terms) declined until the mid-1980s, stabilized for more than a decade, and then began to rise around the turn of the 21st century (figure 2.6). Destination-market concentration fell until the mid-1980s and then rose until the late 1990s, before leveling off and then falling slightly. Both concentration measures are now close to their levels of the early 1960s. Note that even if there has been a greater concentration in destination markets, there has been a substantial shift from exporting commodities to advanced economies to trading instead with emerging economies. For example, the U.S. share as a destination market declined from 44 percent in 1990 to 37 percent in 2008, while China's share rose from 0.8 percent to 10 percent over the same period.

There is, however, a fair degree of heterogeneity in export concentration. For product concentration, Ecuador and República Bolivariana de Venezuela are the least diversified economies, and export concentrations for these two countries were high even in the 1990s, when oil prices fell significantly. By contrast, Argentina has one of the lowest concentration indexes for most of the period analyzed. Colombia seems the most effective country in successfully diversifying its

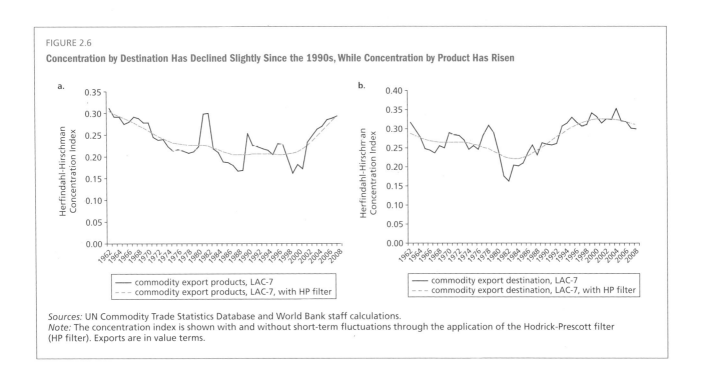

FIGURE 2.6

Concentration by Destination Has Declined Slightly Since the 1990s, While Concentration by Product Has Risen

a.

b.

commodity export products, LAC-7
commodity export products, LAC-7, with HP filter

commodity export destination, LAC-7
commodity export destination, LAC-7, with HP filter

Sources: UN Commodity Trade Statistics Database and World Bank staff calculations.
Note: The concentration index is shown with and without short-term fluctuations through the application of the Hodrick-Prescott filter (HP filter). Exports are in value terms.

export basket, having achieved a huge reduction in the concentration partly as a consequence of a substantial increase in trade openness during the 1990s. In recent years, Colombia has reached the same degree of concentration as Brazil, Mexico, and Peru, countries with a relatively low concentration of exports for the region.

Fact 5: The LAC share of global exports in most commodities is much higher than its economic weight in world GDP. The importance of natural resources for LAC and the significance of LAC in world commodity markets are reflected in its disproportionate share of world commodity exports relative to its economic weight, measured by its contribution to world GDP (figure 2.7). In all but one commodity export category—forestry—the LAC share of world exports remains higher than its economic weight. The disproportion is particularly marked for petroleum, cereals, and tropical exports, where the LAC export share is almost twice its share of global GDP.

Fact 6: The latest global commodity boom (December 2001 to June 2008) was for LAC the longest lasting and most comprehensive in the numbers of commodities affected and countries

benefiting. The effects of this boom and the subsequent decline in prices have heightened interest in the issues addressed in this report. For a sample of 57 commodities over time, 80 percent were in a boom phase in January 2006, the highest since the 85 percent in December 1973. Metals, foods, and agricultural raw materials all boomed starting in early 2002, with oil prices beginning their upturn in December 2001. The latest boom also contrasts with that in the late 1970s, when commodity prices were dominated by short-lived price spikes, particularly for coffee in 1976 and oil in 1974 and 1979. For the 16 commodities most important for the LAC-7 countries, the share in boom was higher, reaching 100 percent in the recent upturn—higher than seen previously in the data—and the broadbased boom lasted considerably longer than those in the past (figure 2.8). Although there was some divergence in the duration of booms in individual countries in the 1970s (with Mexico spending 75 percent of the time from June 1972 to June 1975 in a boom compared with 36 percent for República Bolivariana de Venezuela), all LAC-7 economies

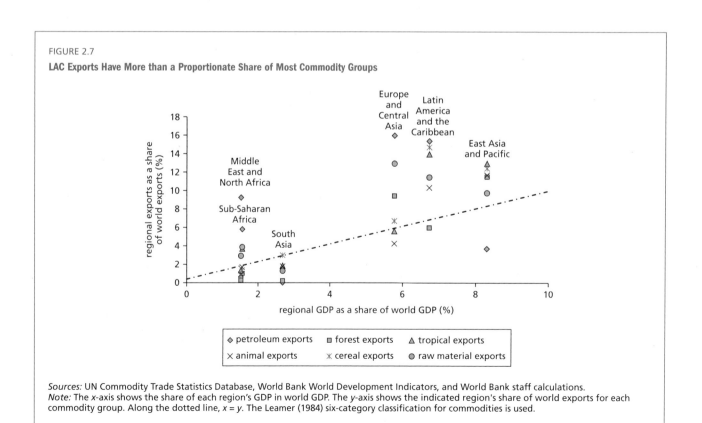

FIGURE 2.7

LAC Exports Have More than a Proportionate Share of Most Commodity Groups

Sources: UN Commodity Trade Statistics Database, World Bank World Development Indicators, and World Bank staff calculations.
Note: The x-axis shows the share of each region's GDP in world GDP. The y-axis shows the indicated region's share of world exports for each commodity group. Along the dotted line, x = y. The Leamer (1984) six-category classification for commodities is used.

FIGURE 2.8

The Latest Boom Was the Most Broad-Based at Least Since Detailed Trade Data Became Available in the Early 1960s

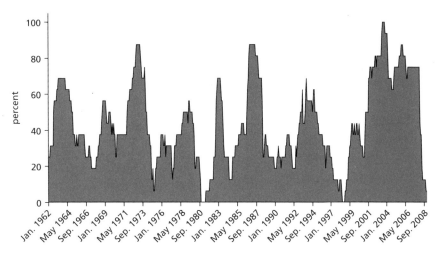

Source: World Bank staff calculations based on export commodity price data from Cunha, Prada, and Sinnott (2009a, 2009b).
Note: The graph represents the share of commodities experiencing a price "boom" for each period of time. This indicator was constructed by aggregating price-boom periods across the top 16 export commodities for the LAC-7 economies, comprising aluminum, beef, coffee, cotton, copper, crude oil, fish, fish meal, gold, iron ore, maize, palm oil, soybeans, soybean oil, sugar, and wheat. Booms and busts in commodity prices were defined following the Bry-Borchan cycle-dating methodology.

FIGURE 2.9

The Recent Boom Brought the Highest Ever Crude Oil Prices and Highest Metals Prices Since WWI, While Real Agricultural Prices Remained Below the Heights of the 1970s

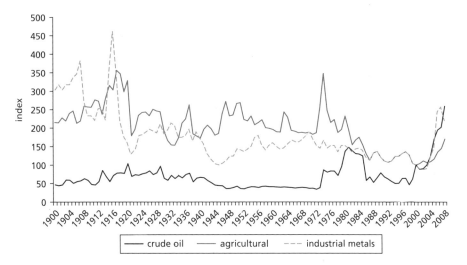

Source: World Bank staff calculations based on Pfaffenzeller, Newbold, and Rayner (2007) commodity weights for agricultural goods and metals.
Note: Agricultural goods and metals price indices calculated using the commodity weights of Grilli and Yang (1988) as set out in Pfaffenzeller, Newbold, and Rayner (2007). "Agricultural" goods consist of bananas, beef, cocoa, coffee, lamb, maize, palm oil, rice, sugar, tea, and wheat. Industrial metals are aluminum, copper, lead, tin, and zinc. Silver is excluded. The manufactures unit value index (MUV) is used to deflate the commodity price indices.

spent close to 90 percent of December 2001 to June 2008 in a boom.

Fact 7: Despite the recent boom, agricultural commodity prices remain well below their 1970s peak. By contrast, oil prices reached historical heights, and metals prices were higher than at any time since 1916 (figure 2.9). So for commodity producing countries as a whole, this episode underscored the volatility of markets. And for hydrocarbon and metals producers, it forced governments to respond to the challenges posed by inflows of foreign exchange that, in the latter half of the boom, were comparable to those in the 1970s. For LAC-7 commodity exports, average real prices in the recent boom remained at half those in the surge of the 1970s, mainly a result of the importance of agricultural goods in the LAC-7 commodity basket.[2] Note, however, that these rising prices do not imply a long-term trend either upward or downward in prices in the future. Econometric analyses show that there have been "structural-break" years where prices have fallen; but apart from these breaks, prices appear to follow a difficult-to-predict random walk, with no clear trend. Current forecasts of the

World Bank are that prices generally are likely to remain at levels above their historical levels, but significantly below recent peaks.

Endnotes

1. Calculations are based on the net commodity price index proposed in Cunha, Prada, and Sinnott (2009a). The values in parentheses represent the percent variation change in prices during the boom relative to the "pre-boom" average. The average index value during the boom (December 2001–June 2008) is compared with its average in the three years prior to the boom (November 1998–November 2001).

2. The recent boom is defined as covering the period from December 2001 to June 2008, while the boom periods of the 1970s cover June 1972 to June 1979.

CHAPTER 3

Natural Resources and Long-Term Growth: Exploring the Linkages

Key messages: As one might intuitively expect, greater natural resource wealth is associated with higher GDP per capita in a cross-country sample. Despite this simple fact, anecdotal evidence and some economic research have called into question whether resources are good or bad for development: that is, whether there is a "natural resource curse." Although the weight of the evidence seems to indicate that, on balance, there is no curse, it is useful to look at some of the individual channels for commodity dependence to allegedly exercise a negative influence. Some seem to be red herrings. We find little support in the evidence for hypotheses that commodities in general have declining price trends relative to manufactures, lower productivity growth, or less potential for linkages and spillovers to the rest of the economy. But the large rents from commodity production undoubtedly can generate Dutch disease effects, with concentrated production and export structures and high fiscal revenue dependence. Commodity prices are also more volatile than manufactures. The evidence that price instability has significant negative effects on welfare or investment, or directly on growth, is weak. But if not managed properly, these fluctuations can be reflected in shocks to the real economy, amplified through procyclical government expenditures and exacerbated by the concentrated structure of production, exports, and fiscal revenues. This, in turn, can compromise growth prospects. Another legitimate concern about resource extraction is that if rents are not reinvested in human or other productive capital, the economy's real stock of wealth will diminish over time.

In this chapter, we consider how commodity production is—and is not—special for its potential and more direct connections to long-term growth. (Indirect effects through institutional channels are considered in chapter IV.) We also consider the legitimate concerns that those special features may elicit. We begin with an overview of the empirical evidence on the relationship between commodity dependence and growth, and then explore a series of specific potential causal channels. The chapter puts some emphasis on Dutch disease—the appreciation of the real exchange rate that commodity exports may generate, especially in booms. But it also explores other channels through which commodity dependence has been alleged to influence growth and economic development, including the dearth of spillovers that commodities are said to generate for other economic activities and the purported secular decline in commodity prices relative to those of manufactures.

A simple correlation between natural capital and GDP, both expressed in per capita terms, seems to confirm the intuition that natural resources contribute to income generation (figure 3.1). Indeed, among the richest countries in the world are the top three in

FIGURE 3.1

Natural Capital per Capita Is Positively Correlated with GDP per Capita

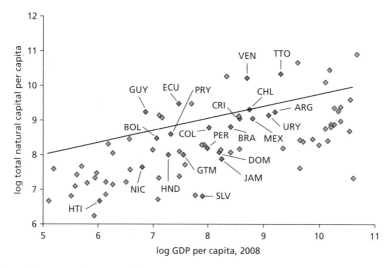

Sources: World Bank World Development Indicators, World Bank Natural Capital Database and World Bank staff calculations.
Note: Resource abundance is measured by the total natural capital per capita in 2000. The log of GDP per capita is based on constant 2000 US$ values. LAC countries are shown as green squares. ARG = Argentina; BOL = Bolivia; BRA = Brazil; COL = Colombia; CRI = Costa Rica; CHL = Chile; DOM = Dominican Republic; ECU = Ecuador; GUY = Guyana; GTM = Guatemala; HTI = Haiti; HND = Honduras; JAM = Jamaica; MEX = Mexico; NIC = Nicaragua; PER = Peru; PRY = Paraguay; SLV = EL Salvador; TTO = Trinidad and Tobago; URY = Uruguay; VEN = República Bolivariana de Venezuela.

natural capital: Norway, New Zealand, and Canada. This overall positive relationship continues to hold for LAC countries (figure 3.1).

Despite this simple and intuitive relationship, a long strand of economic literature has suggested that commodity dependence may hurt a country's growth prospects. Some empirical studies, especially two influential papers by Sachs and Warner (1995, 1997), looked at the relationship between growth and commodity exports' share of total exports or GDP, and seemed to verify a negative impact of natural resources on economic growth. This negative link was dubbed the "natural resource curse." The many examples of resource-rich but income-poor countries seemed to confirm these conclusions, and this hypothesis has become rather generally accepted in journalistic and policy circles. Juan Pablo Perez Alfonzo, a Venezuelan minister of energy and a founder of OPEC, famously declared that "oil is the devil's excrement . . . we are drowning in the devil's excrement." And Moises Naim, the editor-in-chief of *Foreign Policy*, states flatly in a recent (2009) editorial, "Oil is a curse. Natural gas, copper, and diamonds are also bad for a country's health."

Recent economic literature, however, has questioned these findings, particularly the use in empirical work of commodity exports' share of total exports or GDP as a measure of dependence in regressions explaining growth. These measures pose problems of endogeneity in the econometric exercises: there is no way of telling whether countries have been unable to grow because they are so dependent on commodities, or whether they are so dependent on commodities because they have been unable to grow in other sectors. And it turns out—with the use of indicators capturing the exogenously determined degree of commodity "abundance," including variables such as mineral reserves—that the negative relationship between commodity abundance and growth disappears or even emerges as a significantly positive relationship. (See, for example, Lederman and Maloney 2006, 2008;[1] Wright and Czelusta 2004; Brunnschweiler 2008; Stijns 2005; Alexeev and Conrad 2009; Brunnschweiler and Bulte 2008; Sala-i-Martin, Dopelhofer, and Miller 2004.)

Furthermore, it may be a gross overgeneralization to talk about a "natural resource curse" if negative outcomes in resource-abundant countries are mainly confined to those with poor governance (which also has a significant impact on economic growth), or mainly to those with "point-source" resources such as oil and minerals (Collier and Goderis 2007). Others have found evidence of a link between commodity dependence and growth, but operating through indirect channels (van der Ploeg and Poelhekke 2009). Although it is safe to say that there is still no complete consensus on the issue, it would seem that the

case is strong that possessing commodity wealth does not necessarily compromise a country's growth, at least not directly.

But some types of risks may be problematic in some countries or under certain conditions and can undermine economic growth, if natural resources are poorly managed. It is clear that the Dutch disease is real.[2] As economists have noticed for centuries, resource-rich countries do not tend to develop highly diversified economies (see box 3.1).

BOX 3.1

A Brief History of Economic Thought on Dutch Disease

In places where natural resources are abundant—that is, where they can be produced at low cost, relative to the marginal cost of production elsewhere—they generate large profits (economic rents) for the owners. This has two major effects on the relative incentive structure in the economy. First, to the extent the resources are exported, the inflow of foreign exchange appreciates the real exchange rate: that is, it raises the price of nontradable goods relative to that of tradable goods. Second, it increases the returns to production of the resource relative to other tradable goods. Both of these effects reduce the incentive to invest in production of other tradable goods, resulting in a production and export structure concentrated in the resource. Such dynamics are generally referred to as Dutch disease. This terminology is relatively recent, coined in response to the effects on the Dutch economy in the 1970s of oil discoveries in the North Sea, but the concept, broadly defined, was posited much earlier, and it eventually contributed to the evolution of the modern theory of international trade.

The French political philosopher Montesquieu in 1748 stated that in countries where nature easily bestows her bounty, there is little incentive to engage in other, more burdensome productive activities and that this "indolence" leads to the failure of the country to develop. Cairnes (1873) attributed the general underdevelopment of agriculture in Latin America to the region's mineral wealth. To rationalize this observation, he used the standard theory of comparative advantage, basically arguing that the possession of exceptional wealth makes it profitable to satisfy a

country's wants for other goods through international exchange rather than direct domestic production. He also examined the effects of the discovery of gold in Australia in the mid-19th century, where the high money wages brought about by this discovery made it difficult for Australian employers to compete with foreign suppliers of agricultural and industrial goods. Considering that labor is a relatively nontradable primary factor of production, this was, in fact, a description of the phenomenon of real-exchange-rate appreciation.

Later, Wicksell (1916/1958) examined the effects of a sudden increase of the price of a primary commodity on the price of productive factors in Sweden. Wicksell adopted a neoclassical perspective, with differences in factor endowments between countries and differences in factor proportions among sectors. An increase in the international price of land-intensive primary commodities exported by Sweden (such as iron ore and wood) raised the demand and price of the abundant, low-priced factor (land) and reduced the demand and price of the scarce, high-priced factor (labor). This sharp increase in the relative price of the land-intensive commodity suppressed production of other tradables that used it relatively intensively. This observation of the effects of changing relative product prices on relative returns to factors of production was, in fact, a precursor of the Stolper-Samuelson theorem and was further developed by Heckscher (1919/1991) and incorporated into what became known as the Heckscher-Ohlin model, a foundation of the modern theory of international trade.

What is not so clear is whether this is a disease to be cured or a manifestation of comparative advantage that is on balance beneficial. In his descriptions of the Dutch disease effects in Australia, Cairnes (1873) stressed that such changes were not accompanied by a reduction in aggregate income but enabled Australia to enjoy a higher income by participating in foreign trade according to the principles of comparative advantage. And history shows that Australia has become a high-income country, based largely on its resource wealth.

From an economic perspective, the specialization brought about by Dutch disease is a malady only to the extent that devoting a country's real resources to producing commodities is in some way inferior to devoting them to producing something else. This raises the following question: Are commodities different in ways that reduce aggregate growth potential? In several important respects, they are probably not.

Commodity Price Movements Have not followed a Long-Term Trend Relative to Manufactures

One way it has been alleged that commodity production is inferior is the argument by Prebisch and Singer that commodity prices are on a long-term downward trend relative to manufactures, with low rates of productivity improvement. Thus, with terms of trade declining, countries that specialize in their production would fall farther and farther behind economies relying more on manufacturing as an engine of growth. This Prebisch-Singer hypothesis was important in the region's history because it provided an intellectual justification for the import-substitution industrialization strategy many countries adopted in the region until the crises of the 1980s led them to abandon it for outward-oriented policies.

Simple visual inspection of the commodity price index data analyzed by Prebish and Singer (the solid line in figure 3.2, an index of prices of non-oil commodities relative to the manufactures unit value index) seems to show a downward trend. The longer time series from Grilli and Yang may also appear to exhibit a (much weaker) downward trend. But as Cuddington, Ludema, and Jayasuriya (2007) demonstrate, appearances can be deceiving; simulations from a trendless stochastic process can show a strong downward trend.

Sophisticated econometric techniques applied to longer series of actual commodity price indexes than those used by Prebisch and Singer generally fail to indicate such a trend, and the same is true of most individual commodity price series. (See, for example, Balagtas and Holt 2009; Lederman and Maloney 2006; Cuddington, Ludema, and Jayasuriya 2007; and Byrne et al. 2010, who provide reviews of the literature on econometric analysis of these questions as well as some original analysis.) And empirically, it is difficult to account fully for quality improvements over time in manufactured products, implying that when their prices are compared with largely homogeneous commodity prices, the comparison is likely to be biased in favor of showing a relative decline in the latter.

The weight of the empirical evidence seems to indicate that prices are best characterized by a nonstationary process (a random walk), with one or more structural breaks and no long-term trend. Accordingly, after two decades of decline, prices seem to be back at their levels of the 1960s. If it is true that prices follow a random walk, neither the direction nor the size of future price shocks can be predicted, so this cannot be used as the basis for policy. Furthermore, as other observers have noted, even if there is a trend, it is very small relative to the variance, making it of dubious policy concern (Cashin and McDermott 2002).

Productivity trends have been as good for commodities as for other sectors of economic activity

What matters (to producers and to society at large) is profits, not prices. Even if there were a downward trend in prices, as long as producers can stay ahead of the technology curve, they can reduce their costs faster than prices are falling and maintain or even increase profits. And there seems to be little if any systematic evidence that commodity production generally offers more limited opportunities than other activities to take advantage of productivity growth. Consistent with Viner's (1952) early assertion, several empirical investigations (Martin and Mitra 2001; Coelli and Rao 2005; World Bank 2009) have concluded that total factor productivity growth is as high or higher in

FIGURE 3.2

Commodity Prices and the Prebisch-Singer Hypothesis

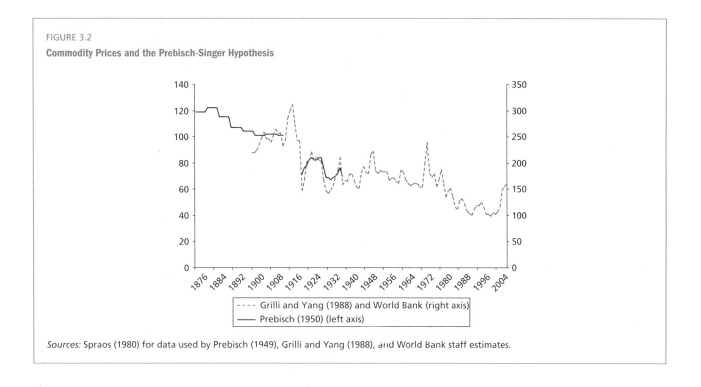

- - - - Grilli and Yang (1988) and World Bank (right axis)
——— Prebisch (1950) (left axis)

Sources: Spraos (1980) for data used by Prebisch (1949), Grilli and Yang (1988), and World Bank staff estimates.

commodity production than in manufactures in a large sample of advanced and developing countries.

Commodity production provides positive "spillovers" and linkages to other sectors, similar to manufacturing

Another critique of commodity production is that it inherently offers fewer positive "spillover" effects for the rest of the economy in creating less potential than other product categories for developing linkages or upgrading to more differentiated, higher-quality, higher-value products. Yet we shall argue that there is no compelling evidence that commodity production is generally "inferior" to other types of production in its linkages and spillovers.

It has long been recognized that industries with forward and backward linkages tend to be good for growth. In a recent strand of economic thought, this has evolved into the idea that countries specializing in products that can serve as "launching pads" for other industries are likely to have better growth prospects. Hausmann, Hwang, and Rodrik (2005) argue that economies grow when their firms or industries move into higher-value-added products through a process of discovering new economic activities in which they can

profitably engage. Thus, firms are better off if they make products closely related to many high-value products in dense areas of the "product space," where it is easier to move from one product to another.[3] Highly productive products in these dense parts of the product space can be empirically identified as those that are commonly exported by higher-income countries. Based on this, they rank product groups with a score ("PRODY"). Countries that export many high-PRODY products would be expected to grow faster. They construct an index ("EXPY") showing how a country's export basket rates on this count, and find that this is indeed correlated with growth in a cross-country sample.

To be sure, Hausmann, Hwang, and Rodrik (2005) do not claim on either theoretical or empirical grounds that natural resource–dependent countries are at an inherent disadvantage in this kind of model.[4] They do note that among the LAC countries in their sample (Argentina, Brazil, Chile, and Mexico), only Mexico has an EXPY score comparable to the East Asian countries. One might take this as evidence that resource-dependent countries are *not* at a disadvantage, because Mexico was once heavily commodity dependent (in 1980, 65 percent of its exports were hydrocarbons), and it has apparently managed to diversify into high-PRODY products. The paper also notes that the variation in EXPY scores among natural resource exporting countries is quite large.

The fact that Chile—one of the highest-performing LAC countries over the last several decades—has a very low and falling EXPY score also may lead to questions about the practical value of this index. Indeed, Lederman and Maloney (2006) find that, if the econometric methodology controls for investment (as a share of GDP) and adds an indicator of export concentration, the correlation disappears between the measures of quality of export portfolio used by Hausmann, Hwang, and Rodrik and overall growth, suggesting that it is diversification, rather than specialization in specific sectors, that is good for growth.

Although Hausmann, Hwang, and Rodrik (2005) never address this question, one might infer from their model that natural resource–based industries would not be good sectors for generating linkages because they remain far from high-value-added and innovative sectors. Such sectors are generally taken to be those in which products are rather highly differentiated and technologically sophisticated, characteristics not associated in popular perception with commodity production.

Yet the popular perception may not be entirely accurate. De Ferranti et al. (2002) described many cases in which mining, forestry, and agriculture have demonstrated a high degree of innovation as well as productivity growth. This can be illustrated by the fact that the quantity of economically useful reserves tends to grow over time through technological innovations in exploration and exploitation.

Furthermore, a detailed study of international trade in metals prepared for this report reveals that these products are indeed differentiated, with intra-industry trade comparable to other sectors (including high-value-added ones) and with good potential to move from low- to high-value products (Mandel 2009). Metal products have a price dispersion—a measure of heterogeneity—comparable to that of footgear and headgear or plastics. Trade in metals is also characterized by a high degree of intra-industry trade, implying the exchange of distinct varieties (figure 3.3). This large heterogeneity in metals creates the potential for specialization in (and upgrading to) more

desirable, higher-quality, higher-value varieties within product categories, as well as moving up the value chain to more processed products. Mandel also found that the market share of newly imported goods is positively and significantly correlated with the new goods' price, implying large increases in the relative quality of those varieties. This "upgrade elasticity" is about equal for metal goods and higher-value-added manufacturing exports.

Overall, LAC seems to have taken advantage of this potential for upgrading: its share of global markets in metals expanded by 175 percent between 1975 and 2004, an annual compound growth rate of 1.9 percent (figure 3.4). Decomposing this increase in share by the stages of the metal production process shows that the overwhelming majority was in the intermediate- and high-value-added categories. The share of both ore and unwrought products roughly doubled over the 30 years. But the share of worked products increased eightfold. Estimates based on value-chain classifications also show that much of the growth can be attributed to LAC moving toward production of more sophisticated and higher-value-added metal products: the fraction of ore trade growth due to upgrades is 0.5; that of unwrought products is 0.64; and that of worked products is 0.43.

Country studies also show extensive increases in value-added, clustering effects, and linkages to other sectors in Chilean (Valdés and Foster 2003) and Argentine (Regunaga 2010) agriculture and in Chilean salmon farming (O'Ryan et al. 2010). Moreover, the popular concept of mines as enclaves with few linkages to local areas is certainly not general. An in-depth study of a Peruvian gold mine found rather extensive linkages through purchases of local labor and other inputs. Each 10 percent increase in the mine's purchases was associated with a 1.7 percent increase in local incomes, with a significant impact on poverty (Aragon and Rud 2009).

Commodity production is also sometimes seen as low-tech, with lower rewards to human capital accumulation. The expectation would be that economies specializing in commodities would not benefit from the positive spillovers from a highly educated population. But evidence from a recent study of the skill premia in

FIGURE 3.3

Intra-Industry Trade in Metals Is Comparable to Other Products

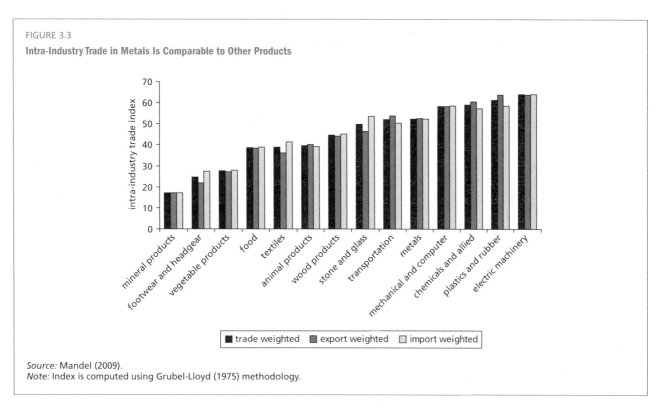

Source: Mandel (2009).
Note: Index is computed using Grubel-Lloyd (1975) methodology.

FIGURE 3.4

LAC's Market Share Has Expanded over Time, Due to Both Inter-Product Upgrading and Intra-Product Quality Improvement

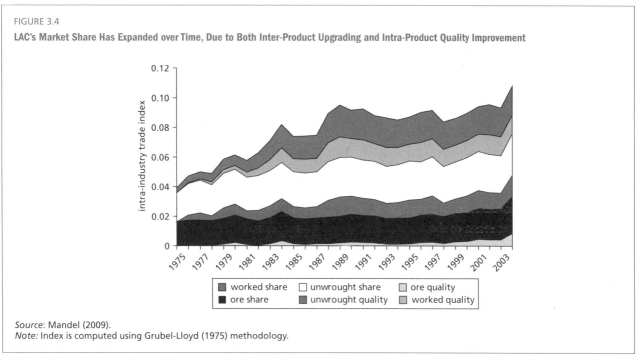

Source: Mandel (2009).
Note: Index is computed using Grubel-Lloyd (1975) methodology.

LAC countries suggests that natural resource industries do not systematically pay less (Brambilla and Porto 2009). Differences were sharp in the average years of education and in the ratios of skilled to unskilled workers. The wage of an employed skilled worker economy-wide is, on average, 53 percent higher than the wage of an employed unskilled worker, but this varies across countries from 38 to 98 percent. As would be expected, a higher percentage of skilled workers in the population tends to lower the skill premium. There are differences in the industry skill premium, both across countries and within a country across industries, and the correlation between exports and industry wage premia is positive. Although the sectoral origin of exports is an important explanator of the skill premium, there is no evidence that commodities rank lower than other sectors on this criterion. Of course, this says nothing about the number of high-skill workers in commodity sectors relative to others, and commodity sectors differ greatly in their labor intensity. But it does show that those workers in commodity production are rewarded as highly.

Given the vast range of products in "commodities," one could not claim that all such products offer the same opportunities as manufacturing for upstream or downstream linkages, quality upgrading, or technological spillovers. To some extent, the opportunities may not be as much a function of the type of commodity as of the economic and institutional environment. In a poor environment, the incentives may favor enclave production with few links, while the opposite may be true in a well-functioning environment. This is true of manufacturing sectors as well, explaining why enclave-like export processing zones can sometimes succeed in countries with poor business environments. Exactly how the institutional environment influences the type of production structure that develops for exploiting resource wealth is a subject for further research. But the discussion here shows that commodity production on average is not inherently inferior to other sectors. Even so, commodities differ from other production in several ways, and some create special risks.

Commodity Production Generates Large Rents, Making Countries Susceptible to Dutch Disease

Commodity production (especially minerals and hydrocarbons) is often associated with large rents, which cause large inflows of foreign exchange, which tend to discourage diversification to noncommodity exportable or import-competing goods. To the extent that commodity production does not inherently generate lower economic growth through the channels previously mentioned, specialization in these products would not seem to be a

source of concern. But some evidence indicates that a concentration of exports in and of itself—be it in commodities or other products—may reduce long-term growth (Lederman and Maloney 2009). One reason for this may be that concentrating exports in fewer products implies more volatile terms of trade (a topic discussed in more detail in the following section), which increases output variability and reduces growth (Jansen 2004). Lederman and Xu (2009) use a cross-section of 158 countries with data from 1980 to 2005 to test each link in the chain of causation individually—from commodity concentration to export concentration, from export concentration to terms-of-trade volatility, and from terms-of-trade volatility to output volatility. They conclude that each of these links seems to hold.

If Dutch disease causes concentration, and concentration reduces growth through the chain just described, one might reasonably conclude that there could well be a negative connection between commodity dependence and growth. But the empirical evidence cited earlier on this relationship has been ambiguous. Recent studies find that commodity abundance has either a positive effect or no effect on growth. (The multistage causal link has not been much investigated, with the exception of Lederman and Xu, who did not make the final connection to growth.) One possible explanation of this apparent paradox could be that though the connection at each stage is significant in a statistical sense, there is so much "noise" in each link that the overall connection is too weak to detect. This could be a worthwhile topic for future investigation. Or it could be that the direct benefits of commodity wealth outweigh the concentration effect.

Prices are less stable

Although comparisons are difficult, it seems that commodities are different in that their prices are more volatile than those of manufactures (figure 3.5). As Angus Deaton (1999, p. 27) once put it: "What commodities lack in trend, they make up for in variance." At least since the time of Keynes, economists have been concerned about this instability of commodity prices and its effect on the investment and growth prospects of developing countries because of risk and uncertainty.

FIGURE 3.5

The Price Volatility of Commodities Is Higher Than That of Manufactures

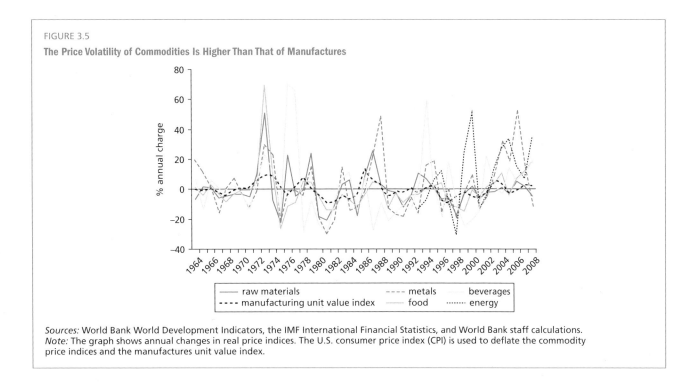

Sources: World Bank World Development Indicators, the IMF International Financial Statistics, and World Bank staff calculations.
Note: The graph shows annual changes in real price indices. The U.S. consumer price index (CPI) is used to deflate the commodity price indices and the manufactures unit value index.

This led Keynes to propose a third institution (in addition to the International Monetary Fund and the World Bank)—"Commod Control"—to stabilize commodity markets. This proposal was followed in 1974 by a call from the UN Secretariat for an Integrated Program for Commodities, including stockpiling schemes for major commodities, price support, and a facility to help countries offset temporary export earning shocks. Neither Commod Control nor the Integrated Program ever became operational, although elements of the proposals were incorporated in the UN's Common Fund for Commodities[5] and the IMF's Compensatory Finance Facility.

A long line of models and empirical investigations of the relationship between price volatility, on the one hand, and investment, welfare, and growth on the other have produced ambiguous results. Early models, beginning with Waugh's (1944) seminal piece, focused on partial-equilibrium measures of consumer and producer welfare under stable versus unstable prices. Newbery and Stiglitz (1981) reviewed this literature and analyzed the benefits and costs of international price stabilization schemes of the kind recommended by Keynes. They extended previous models to include benefits of stabilization flowing from risk aversion—focusing on the fact that income risk, not price risk, matters to producers. They concluded that previous studies had overestimated the benefits, which they estimated to be (depending on the commodity and degree of risk aversion) between 1 and 6 percent of revenues for some agricultural commodities commonly exported by developing economies. In the end, they "question seriously the desirability of price stabilization schemes both from the point of view of the producer and that of the consumer" (p. 23). But they were more agnostic in their consideration of possible macroeconomic benefits.

Later research focused on the effects of price volatility on investment. Knudsen and Parnes (1975) pointed out that uncertainty may increase the incentives for saving, which translates into more investment in a model with no international capital flows. But Newbery and Stiglitz (1981)—using a different model, also with no international capital flows—showed that instability could either increase or decrease investment. Acemoglu and Zilibotti (1997) argued that riskiness of investment projects would bias investment toward low-risk, low-return projects, but their model was based on investment flows between two "large" economies, with savers in both exhibiting risk-averse behavior. Nash (1990) considered a volatile commodity-dependent small economy with an open-capital account. He concluded that domestic savers in such a country can invest abroad in relatively low-risk assets, leaving the risky commodity-related domestic investments to foreign investors, who are less risk averse. So, neither savings nor investment should be systematically depressed by risk. This was confirmed in a sample of countries with open-capital accounts. It seems reasonable to suppose, therefore, that this link between price volatility and investment is of less concern in today's world of integrated capital markets than it was in Keynes's time.

Price fluctuations, regardless of their effect on investment, create volatility in foreign exchange earnings and government revenues. Indeed, fiscal revenues from resources are much more variable than those from other sources (figure 5.2). This complicates macroeconomic management, to which we return later. Volatile fiscal revenues and associated procyclical spending could have real costs for growth by lowering the efficiency of public spending and generating shocks to the real economy. Empirically, instability is associated with real output variability (di Giovanni and Levchenko 2009; Rodrik 1997). And a long line of research has connected output volatility to lower growth in cross-country samples (Ramey and Ramey 1995; Hausmann and Gavin 1996; Easterly and Kraay 2000; Fatás 2002; Fatás and Mihov 2003; Hnatkovska and Loayza 2005; Loayza et al. 2007). A recent empirical paper by van der Ploeg and

Poelhekke (2009) tries to separate the direct impact of natural resources on growth—which the authors find may very well be positive—from the indirect effect resulting from the increased volatility in economic output, which they find to be negative.

Some commodities are exhaustible

Another special characteristic of some commodities—particularly minerals and hydrocarbons—is that they are exhaustible. So if a country's natural wealth is extracted and not replaced by some other durable capital, total wealth will decline, and growth will not be sustained. There is some evidence that this has been the case for some LAC countries.

One simple and intuitive rule for ensuring that development is sustainable—in the sense that real welfare will not decline—is the "Hartwick rule" that all rents from natural resource extraction should be reinvested in some other form of capital, either human or physical. Table 3.1 displays the percentages by which physical capital would have increased if countries in the region had followed two sustainability rules: the Hartwick rule (column 2) and an augmented Hartwick rule (column 3), investing an amount equal to a constant 5 percent of GDP. The first column of table 3.1 shows the results of an exercise estimating produced capital using actual investment time series. The three estimates of produced capital start from a common initial stock of capital. Positive entries show that the region's or country's

TABLE 3.1

Differences between Capital Stock Estimated from Actual Investment Data and Counterfactuals
(percent)

Region	(1) Produced capital in 2006 (billions of 2005 US$)	(2) Hartwick rule	(3) Augmented Hartwick rule	(4) Rent/GDP average, 1979–2006 (percent)
Latin America and Caribbean	5,428	13.8	59.8	7.2
East Asia and Pacific	8,144	−68.0	−48.0	5.9
Middle East and North Africa	1,375	70.3	102.8	20.6
South Asia	2,332	−61.1	−28.7	3.3
Sub-Saharan Africa	999	88.5	139.9	12.3
High-income: OECD	70,210	−37.0	6.6	1.3
World	89,539	−34.6	6.5	2.3

Source: Ram and Ruta (2009).

actual capital stock is below what it would have been if it had followed the sustainability rule—in other words, they show that the region or country is "running down" its real wealth.[6]

The simulations suggest that, as of 2006, Latin America and the Caribbean would have had Hartwick rule capital 13.8 percent higher than the actual level. Several LAC economies would have produced capital above the actual levels—some very substantially above, including República Bolivariana de Venezuela (257 percent), Suriname (153 percent), and Bolivia (135 percent). Had the augmented saving rule been followed, investment would have been higher each year than the Hartwick rule investment, resulting in a capital stock 59.8 percent higher regionwide. As we discuss in more detail below, this failure to invest the proceeds of resource extraction can be ascribed to rentier effects, which cause governments to dissipate much of the rent in unproductive spending. A similar conclusion can be reached for the Middle East and North Africa and for Sub-Saharan Africa. By contrast, East Asia and the Pacific and South Asia have invested over time more than these simple saving rules suggest, resulting in an actual capital stock higher than the counterfactuals.

On balance, we conclude that much of the literature on the links between resource dependence and growth has been overly pessimistic and, to some extent concerned with the wrong links. Although there are potential downsides, they come not from secularly declining prices or features of commodity production that make it inferior as an engine of growth. Instead, they come more from the effects on macroeconomic stability, exacerbated by concentrating exports. This suggests two major points of intervention to break the potential negative chain of causality between commodity dependence and growth: diversifying production and managing government revenues.

The feasibility and success of the two interventions depend, however, on the ability and willingness of governments to manage economic policy well. This introduces a factor silent until now, but one that could represent a key channel through which commodity production could negatively affect economic growth: institutional quality. One major concern about commodity dependence is that it may corrode the very institutions needed to take full advantage of resource wealth. To these issues we now turn.

Endnotes

1. Lederman and Maloney also find that even using the same measure of resource abundance as Sachs and Warner, the curse vanishes when they either (1) treat two outliers, which Sachs and Warner adjust in a way different from the rest of the data points, in a manner consistent with the other data, or (2) modify all the data the way Sachs and Warner modify the two outliers.

2. Classic papers on Dutch disease include Gregory (1976), Corden and Neary (1983), Corden (1984), Eastwood and Venables (1982), and Enders and Herberg (1983).

3. They liken this to monkeys jumping from tree to tree in the forest. Monkeys are better off in dense areas, where trees are close together.

4. Nor does Rodrik, in his more policy-oriented related piece (2004).

5. Founded in 1989, it is still operational, mainly as an advocacy and funding agency for commodity development, with headquarters in Amsterdam (www.common-fund.org).

6. A caveat is in order. The estimates of actual produced capital in table 3.1 (column 1) are based on the assumption that what has not been set aside as gross fixed-capital formation has been consumed. To the extent that a country has been saving rents in financial assets, the comparison in columns 2 and 3 would tend to overestimate the difference between counterfactual and actual levels of capital. This, for example, would be true in the case of Chile, which has placed a significant portion of its copper earnings in financial assets.

CHAPTER 4

Institutions and the Resource Curse or Blessing

Key messages: The varied development outcomes associated with natural resource abundance are often explained as resulting from differences in institutional quality. However, convincing empirical evidence that the natural resource curse is conditional on the quality of institutions has not yet emerged from cross-country studies. Moving beyond the averages, an abundance of country experience points to the risks for social and economic development when resource booms are accompanied by perverse institutional and political economy effects.

At the core of the institutional story is the potential for large and volatile rents—most often from minerals, particularly oil—to corrupt the political process, leading to patronage, rent seeking, and (at the extreme) political instability and violent conflict. To manage natural resources and these rents—subject as they are to volatility—the government must make a credible commitment to citizens to use these endowments well over time. When politicians serve for short horizons and credible commitments are difficult, natural resource outcomes are likely to be problematic. There have certainly been many instances in LAC history when resource rents motivated autocratic behavior or corrupted institutional control of spending during a boom, leading to desolation in the ensuing bust. But compared with other developing regions, LAC has escaped the worst. Rent seeking and dissipation are not that bad in many countries. Nationalization of resources has been less problematic than elsewhere. And oil and mining rents have not quashed democracy or led to violent conflict. The explanation may lie in the ability of LAC society to act collectively to punish bad behavior by governments. Where citizens can discipline politicians, governments are less likely to renege on policy commitments.

As with Dutch disease, institutional explanations of the failure of natural resource abundance to deliver sustained growth have a long history in the economic literature.[1] The basic argument is that natural resources can poison institutions—possibly more when resource discoveries and booms materialize when the country's institutions are already deficient— and weak institutions can in turn undermine growth.[2] Enclave mining or plantation agriculture may not require much institutional development, but may accommodate well to environments with poor governance and substantial shortfalls in the rule of law. They may even reinforce a bad equilibrium of deficient institutions.

In particular, poor institutions may foster exploitation of natural resources that does not rely on sophisticated contractual environments. Under these circumstances, the demand for institutional change may be low because the benefits of marginal institutional improvements would be smaller than where resource exploitation relies on complex and efficient contractual environments (e.g., when resource exploitation is associated with significant clustering of related economic activities, substantial forward and backward linkages, and robust networks and spillover effects). A bad equilibrium can thus develop: weak institutions lead to natural resource exploitation patterns that do not call for better institutions, keeping institutions deficient and undermining growth.[3]

Without a major leap in institutional quality, institution-poor but resource-rich countries might not be able to break free to a good equilibrium where resource wealth, good institutions, and growth reinforce one another (Vardy 2010; see box 4.1). This reasoning is consistent with the theory of rent cycling, which stresses that initial conditions determine whether the "curse" will materialize, highlighting the existence of institutional quality thresholds below which natural resource discoveries harm a country's development path (Auty 1993).[4]

Empirical work has not yet teased out convincing evidence that the natural resource curse is worse with low-quality institutions. To be sure, Mehlum, Moene, and Torvik (2006)—in cross-country econometric work that uses primary exports as a share of GNI as the proxy for resource abundance—do find that a low-growth curse is associated with more resource abundance in countries with poor institutions, whereas countries with high institutional quality neutralize the curse. This result, however, is not robust to changes in specification. In particular, it does not hold when better measures of resource abundance are used to avoid the endogeneity problem posed by their proxy—that a high share of primary exports in national income may itself be the result of low growth.

In fact, some studies provide evidence that the growth benefits of natural resource abundance are greater, on average, for countries with weak institutions (see, for instance, Alexeev and Conrad 2009; Brunnschweiler 2008). As explained by Brunnschweiler (2008), a negative interaction between resource abundance and institutional quality may be due to a "convergence effect." Countries with lower institutional and economic development over the sample period

(1970–2000) benefited more in growth from an abundance of natural resources simply because they were catching up, having started from lower development. The difficulty in establishing an empirical interaction between institutions and natural resources is consistent with the more general result in recent research described in chapter 3: there is no consistent empirical support in favor of the "curse," contrary to the famous claim by Sachs and Warner (1995, 1997).

Beyond the inconsistent results from cross-country empirical work that capture the connections between institutions and natural resource wealth, the fact remains that resource-abundant countries may become entangled in a web of perverse institutional and political economy effects that can undercut sustained social, political, and economic progress. These risks are exemplified by many historical instances in Latin America. There, commodity bonanzas (cocoa, rubber, bananas, silver) in countries with underdeveloped institutions led to feverish expansions only to be followed by long periods of economic stagnation, and even desolation, when the price of the previously booming commodity took a nosedive.

With this downside in mind, the rest of this chapter focuses on the main channel for commodity abundance to affect institutions: rentier effects. We begin by setting out the characteristics of natural resources that lead to the rentier problem and by discussing the main mechanisms whereby natural resources to affect economic and political outcomes. Next, we turn to evidence from LAC on the dissipation of windfall rents from natural resources. Then we discuss some of the dynamics behind the oft-observed cycle of nationalization-privatization of natural resource industries. Last, we examine the evidence from LAC on ways for dependence to adversely affect the development of democratic political institutions or to lead to social conflict. This is not an exhaustive treatment of the institutional aspects of the resource curse. But in limiting our analysis to a discrete set of issues, we hope to shed light on some critical channels through which volatile and large natural resource rents have affected and may continue to affect institutions and the policy-making process in LAC.

BOX 4.1

No Exit? How a Country May Get Stuck in a Bad Institution Trap

In a theoretical model of endogenous institutional development prepared for this report, countries may fall into a low-level inescapable institutional trap (Vardy 2010). In that model, institutional quality is represented by contract enforcement. If institutional quality is high, it is cheap to enforce contracts. Improving institutional quality is costly, and institutions will be improved if and only if the benefits of doing so outweigh this cost. Production of a widget requires many steps, and there are gains from specialization. Thus, the most efficient way to produce widgets where contract enforcement is efficient is with many firms, each specializing in one step in the process.

This will be the situation in a country with reasonably good institutions to begin with. Because the benefits of institutional improvement are more or less proportional to the number of transactions, the benefits will be high in such a country, and there will be pressure for further improvement. Thus, the country is in a virtuous cycle, with its institutions getting continually better over time.

This is not so, however, in a country that starts out with poor institutions. In this country, widgets are produced with only a few companies in the production chain. Here, with few transactions, the benefits to a marginal improvement in institutional quality are small, perhaps too small to outweigh the costs. So, in the absence of some kind of "big push," this country will be stuck in a low-level equilibrium. One can relate this situation to enclave production of commodities, in which, for example, a mining company provides all its own services, bringing in much of its personnel from outside the country.

There is no source for an endogenous big push in this model, but in the real world, things may not be so hopeless. Many exogenous forces could overcome barriers to institutional reform, including pressure for change from those not benefiting from the current institutional arrangements. Anything that lowers the cost of improving institutions (technological advances, outside assistance, contestability) or increases perceptions of the value of improving institutions (longer time horizons so that a higher value of future benefits could be weighed against the current one-time cost of overcoming barriers) can also work to promote change. Finally, the very volatility of commodity prices could lead to an economic crisis, a propitious time for institutional reform.

Source: Vardy (2010).

Commodity Dependence and "Rentier" Effects

The concept of the rentier state was popularized by Mahdavy (1970) to describe the situation in pre-revolutionary Pahlavi Iran. He argued that a government receiving significant oil revenues from abroad tends to become autocratic and unaccountable to its own citizens. Rentier effects are thus associated with a high proportion of government revenue originating from resource rents. Rents from natural resources tend to be large, volatile, geographically concentrated, and controlled by the government. The consequent fiscal volatility may create an unfortunate political dynamic that ratchets up expenditures in booms to levels that cannot be efficiently absorbed or sustained over time, with a stop-go pattern of public expenditure that reduces the quality of public investment and services and thus limits growth potential.

The geographic concentration of natural resource sites, moreover, tends to create pressures to decentralize revenue toward local governments in those sites. This is not necessarily bad since resource extraction can have undesirable environmental and social consequences for which local jurisdictions need to be compensated. But to the degree that local institutions are less capable than the central government and do not internalize the national interest to the same extent, decentralization of revenues unduly dominated by the location of the natural resource site can degrade spending quality. Moreover large rents create a valuable "prize," setting up incentives to contest for political power, perhaps even violently. It is this set of issues that is explored here.

Not all natural resources are equally associated with rentier effects. What matters is the size of the rents and the ease with which the government may appropriate them. Hydrocarbon and mineral natural resources are most closely associated with large rents—oil more than gas or metals. Economic rents do not generally emerge in agriculture, fisheries, or forestry, with rare exceptions arising from temporary perturbations in supply. Another characteristic for differentiating natural resources is the ease of taxing them. Point-source resources—hydrocarbon and large mining operations—are more easily taxed. Production of other commodities, including most agricultural products, is more geographically diffuse, leading to lower profit margins, and involves a wider range of private actors.[5] Taxing these natural resources may therefore be much like taxing other production activities, which, when not incorporating rents, involves economic distortions and political costs.

The central problem of rents is the ability—or inability—of political actors to credibly commit to using natural resource revenues optimally for the public's welfare over time. For example, the volatility of rents poses the problem of whether a government can credibly pledge to save today to spend tomorrow. When credible commitment is difficult and policy horizons are short, those in political power place little value on putting away natural resource revenues for future consumption, and rent dissipation is more likely. The capture of political parties or governments by relatively narrow class groupings or sectoral interests could be prevented if the government could make a credible commitment to a wider group of potential supporters. Societal pressures that extend the planning horizon of politicians and punish the misuse of rents—a sort of social pact to use rents for the best interests of society—would make the emergence of such a credible commitment more likely. Governments are more prone to make such credible commitments when reneging is costly. Otherwise, a lack of trust in leaders to use resource rents well can create greater incentives for citizens to engage in rent seeking or to attempt to broker political power for patronage to gain their "fair" share.

Rentier effects on economic management

Government coffers replete with natural resource rents are tempting targets, with a number of possible corrosive effects on public institutions.

Patronage

Controlling resource rents creates a significant payoff for those with political power but also increases the payoff for contesting that power. At the extreme, the incidence of coups or civil wars could be increased if the rents raise the payoff for staging a coup beyond the costs associated with failure of the coup (Dunning 2009; Ross 2010). But in a more moderate form, patronage can lead to an inefficient allocation of resources, hurting economic growth. The increased payoff to staying in power from commodity rents can induce the government to spend more resources to improve its chances of staying in power or of being reelected. This can easily involve patronage through the targeting of government expenditures at key constituencies, whether by expanding public employment or investing in politically expedient "pork barrel" projects. Increasing the value of political officeholding could also have beneficial effects by extending the planning horizon of politicians, resulting in more productive uses of resource rents and a better path of resource extraction (Kolstad and Wiig 2009).

Rent seeking

The pot of rents also has the demand-side effect of potential beneficiaries of government largesse, resulting in rent-seeking behavior. Rent seeking results in a waste of real resources, as economic agents spend time and other resources on nonproductive activities "to win a contestable prize" (Drazen 2000) and capture the rents (Lane and Tornell 1996; Tornell and Lane 1999; Baland and Francois 2000; Torvik 2002).

Rent-seeking models focus on private individuals outside the government who have the choice of engaging in productive or rent-seeking activities. Rent-seeking activities can be legal—for example, through lobbying—or illegal and corrupt, such as through bribery or extortion. In booms, the windfall gain can boost demand for fiscal resources from powerful groups. Where multiple powerful groups exist and the legal-political institutional infrastructure is weak, there can be what Tornell and Lane (1999) term a "voracity effect"—a more-than-proportional increase in discretionary fiscal spending in response to a positive revenue shock, such as an oil revenue windfall. The national government is typically the recipient of hydrocarbon and mineral windfall revenues; therefore the most expedient way for powerful groups to appropriate the windfall is through the budgetary process. But the increased fiscal transfers to multiple powerful groups can cause government spending to rise by an amount exceeding the windfall revenues. When fiscal spending is not productive, there can be a negative impact on growth.

Incentives for patronage and rent seeking can exist even if resource-related revenues are stable. But the cyclical nature of these revenues can combine with pressure for increased spending and exacerbate the problem, fostering procyclicality in fiscal policy and associated ratcheting of public spending.

It should be clear from this discussion that mitigating the corrosive rentier effects of natural resource abundance constitutes a significant challenge for public policy, institutions, and political processes. Certain features of institutional arrangements and policy-making processes can help to meet this challenge, including well-designed systems of checks and balances, high degrees of transparency and accountability, and society's ability to develop a "state policy" on managing natural resource wealth that is sustained despite electoral changes. These features lead to a greater probability that political actors will credibly commit to optimal intertemporal use of natural resources.

Countries with a prudent spending response to commodity-related revenue windfalls also tend to be more resistant to patronage and rent-seeking activities. In these countries, politicians have been able to credibly commit to appropriate management of natural resource rents over time. Although certain institutional and political economy characteristics make the emergence of such a societal pact more likely, other factors contribute as well, such as the learning effects associated with reaping the rewards of sound economic management resulting from the availability of countercyclical fiscal resources in bad times (see chapter 7).

In LAC, Chile has the least propensity toward profligacy in spending rents, much of which can be explained by institutional features. Copper rents, controlled by the national government, are managed transparently, with technical rules governing the identification and spending of windfall revenues. Excessive contention by political parties and their clienteles over rents has been curbed in Chile by a broad consensus between the modern left coalition (Concertación) and opposition parties on the need to maintain a countercyclical fiscal policy and generate long-term savings from the copper boom. Similarly, Norway has been successful in managing the fiscal policy implications of oil revenues. Davis, Ossowski, and Fedelino (2003) identify its mature democracy and strong, consensus-oriented parliamentary institutions as key factors behind this outcome. The country benefits from a broad societal understanding of the need to restrain public spending and avoid volatile expenditure patterns. Transparent political and bureaucratic processes and stable policies that incorporate long-term considerations contribute to the prudent fiscal outcomes.

Prudence and long time horizons for managing windfall commodity rents are arguably easier to achieve where private enterprise thrives. A strong and efficient private sector that perceives broad opportunities to engage in productive enterprise is less likely to engage in rent-seeking activities. Baland and Francois (2000) present a model with multiple equilibria in which a resource boom can either increase or decrease the proportion of the population engaged in entrepreneurship (productive activity), depending on initial conditions.[6] When a resource boom occurs, the opportunity cost to individuals who engage in rent seeking is forgone productive activity (entrepreneurship). In the authors' framework, the greater the proportion of entrepreneurs in a country when a resource discovery or boom hits, the higher the initial returns are to entrepreneurship. Therefore, a strong initial industrial base decreases rent seeking by making it less lucrative.

Rent dissipation in LAC

The procyclical fiscal policy response to business cycle movements has been established in empirical studies for Latin America (Gavin and Perotti 1997; Alesina, Campante, and Tabellini 2008). A key culprit may be the procyclical government spending response often associated with commodity price booms and busts. This section examines the evidence on rent dissipation in LAC and the possible role of patronage and rent seeking.[7] The evidence points to the existence of effects such as those discussed by Cuddington (1989), who points out that while booms tend to be accompanied by unsustainable increases in public sector spending, once the boom ends, governments are slow to reduce spending, not least because of rigidities and costs to reversal. Besides providing the state with a pot of resources that can be used to mobilize political support, windfall rents may incite myriad private interests to clamor for public spending. This may take the form of subsidies for energy consumption, increased pensions, contracts for infrastructure construction, and so on (Webb 2010).

There is a necessary overlap between the discussion here and that of the next section, which covers the fiscal response to the recent commodity price cycle in more detail. Here, the treatment is selective and in no way attempts to provide a thorough account of country experiences during the latest boom in LAC. Country studies commissioned for this report provide detail on the political economy aspects of the recent boom in Bolivia, Chile, Ecuador, and Trinidad and Tobago.[8] This section summarizes the evidence from these country studies, without attempting to rank or accurately measure the quantitative consequences for the economy of patronage and rent-seeking behavior in individual countries. The discussion is illustrative only, and the conclusions should not be generalized to the region.

Energy subsidies are a key avenue that LAC countries use to dissipate resource rents to domestic consumers. Subsidizing energy is not unique to LAC commodity-exporting countries; the governments of many small commodity-import-reliant economies also subsidize energy consumption. Nevertheless, the large commodity exporters feature prominently among the countries that provide substantial energy subsidies, principally subsidies on the consumer prices of fuels but also on the price of electricity (figure 4.1). In 2005, energy subsidies in LAC equaled, on average, 2.1 percent of GDP, ranging from 0.1 percent in Chile to 8.7 percent in República Bolivariana de Venezuela (OLADE 2007). Oil exporters Ecuador and República Bolivariana de Venezuela had the largest energy price subsidies as a percent of GDP, in the range of 7–8 percent.

Nondiscriminatory energy price subsidies are very regressive: they favor those who consume more energy in absolute terms, typically more affluent individuals and organizations. The case of fuel and liquefied petroleum gas (LPG) subsidies in Ecuador illustrates this point. Some 85 percent of the gasoline subsidy in Ecuador benefits the richest quintile of the population (SIISE-STFS 2003; World Bank–IADB 2004). In 2007, the benefit was US$1,053 for an average family in the richest quintile but only US$173 for a family in the poorest quintile. Fuel subsidies in Ecuador, moreover, create incentives for wasteful overconsumption; a

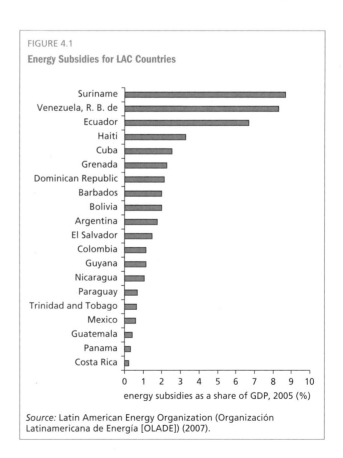

FIGURE 4.1

Energy Subsidies for LAC Countries

Source: Latin American Energy Organization (Organización Latinamericana de Energía [OLADE]) (2007).

well-known example is rich households building gas-heated swimming pools that are much larger than they would be if prices more closely reflected the social opportunity cost of gas and other fuels.

Energy subsidies in Ecuador, on average, cost double what the country spends on education. Indeed, Ram and Ruta (2009) point out that for a number of LAC countries, the fiscal cost of energy price subsidies is higher than the resources allocated to education: education spending in LAC ranges from 2 to 5 percent of GDP, whereas energy subsidies reach as high as 8.7 percent (in Suriname). Moreover, energy subsidies are not transparent, obscuring the budgetary trade-offs. Generally, the fiscal cost of subsidies is not made explicit in budgets. Again, take the example of Ecuador. The public accounts provide no direct record of fuel subsidies; rather, this cost is only implicit in the difference between the state-owned oil company Petroecuador's expenses and revenues. The hidden subsidy reflects the forgone income from crude oil used in local refining that could have been exported at the international price, on the one hand, and the losses from selling refined products at a much lower price than the cost of importing them or producing them at home, on the other.

Rent capture also takes place within the public sector

Organizations within the public sector—in LAC, most notably state-owned enterprises, public sector workers, subnational governments, and on occasion the military—can push to benefit from resource rents. In effect, the public sector is made up of a collection of organized groups, some of which press to get larger allocations of rents (Buchanan and Tullock 1962; North et al. 2007). Medas and Zakharova (2008) document how some Latin American countries have used the recent oil revenue windfall to raise public sector wages disproportionately. This has been the case, for example, in Bolivia and in Trinidad and Tobago, in connection with their hydrocarbons income, and in Argentina, in connection with its agricultural commodity boom. In Trinidad and Tobago, windfall rents continued to flow to urban unions, particularly the civil service, which received a large pay increase in 2003 following a change in government.

There is evidence that the military in some countries has also gained disproportionately during the recent commodity price boom. Thus, for Mexico, Webb (2010) documents that oil exports have been a prominent source of revenue for the military, in addition to considerable benefits meted out to PEMEX employees. In Chile, the military receives the equivalent of 10 percent of CODELCO sales, sharing significantly in the windfall in a way that enhances the military's independence from the budget game.[9]

Substantial rents go to subnational governments in LAC

Subnational governments in LAC receive and spend a sizable share of natural resource rents. Argentina, Bolivia, Brazil, Colombia, Ecuador, Mexico, and República Bolivariana de Venezuela all have revenue-sharing systems that earmark a large share of natural resource revenues for states, regions, and municipalities. Pressures to obtain more advantageous revenue-sharing arrangements by localities where natural resources are exploited may be particularly strong—and understandably so—in regions populated by socially marginalized and minority ethnic groups that have been the victims of a long history of exclusion. But pure political patronage can also often be at play. Diaz-Cayeros (2009), for example, draws attention to the patronage networks in Mexico financed by oil revenue (excedentes petroleros) captured by governors.

Sharing commodity windfall revenues with subnational governments where the commodity is produced or extracted is not in itself the problem. This sort of spending could be required in an effort to mitigate damages to the local population or the environment from resource production activities or to correct long-standing inequalities affecting ethnic groups or traditionally excluded populations. But taken to the extreme, the argument that the body governing the location that generates the revenue should receive it back proportionally to the amounts generated would eliminate the social gains from coordinated production of public goods and services in the national interests, including stabilization and equity-driven compensation services.

Moreover, where subnational governments lack the institutional capacity to spend their allocations of natural resource rents efficiently, funds may be wasted. The institutional quality of national and subnational governments may vary, and thus, so may the social return on the spending of resource revenues at each level of government. There is evidence that resource rents at the subnational level are often linked to poor-quality spending and a rise in rent seeking. This suggests that decentralization of resource rents is risky and must be accompanied by capacity building at the subnational level.

Indeed, windfall rents may exacerbate the quality of subnational institutions, as two recent papers on Brazil show. Caselli and Michaels (2009) find that the oil-driven increases in municipal revenues and reported spending have not been accompanied by a commensurate improvement in the welfare of people living in the municipalities. In particular, the increase in municipal spending was not matched by a corresponding increase in the provision of public goods and services, as recorded by household survey–based measures. Observed increases in household income associated with royalty-induced government revenues were found to be negligible. Where, then, did the oil revenues go? The authors find evidence that they went disproportionately to municipal employees and were partly accounted for by some degree of rent seeking and corruption. Brollo, Nannicini, Perotti, and Tabellini (2010) find empirical evidence that the large windfall transfers to Brazilian municipalities seem to have induced more political corruption (as measured by a random audit program).

Yet these negative local effects are not inevitable. Outcomes depend on complex interactions among institutional quality, administrative capacity, and policies. Thus, Perry and Olivera (2009), using data from 32 departments and 1,098 municipalities in Colombia, find that higher-quality institutions—particularly those related to property rights—help reduce the natural resource curse and reinforce the positive effects of natural resource production and royalties at the regional level. The same effect appears, although in a weaker form, in departments where there is more transparent administrative (especially audit)

institutions and with the maturity of civil-society organizations in municipalities.

Who's Running the Show? Management of Natural Resource Sectors

It is important to ensure that the natural resource sector contributes its full potential to economic growth. Economic historians have shown the critical role of resource-based industries and revenues in the early stages of development of now high-income countries, including the United States. In a seminal contribution, Wright (1990) argues that the exploitation of natural resources was instrumental in the emergence of the United States as the world's preeminent manufacturing nation during 1879-1940. Institutions and government policies had much to do with this. He finds that resource abundance reflected greater exploration and exploitation of geological potential, not just the initially known geological endowment. David and Wright (1997) argue that the factors that made possible the rapid exploitation of mineral deposits in the United States were mostly related to institutions and supportive government policies and included an accommodating legal environment, investment in public knowledge (such as geological surveys), and educational advances in mining, minerals, and metallurgy.

One critical factor is ownership. In the development of natural resources, the requirement of large up-front investments, among other things, creates pressure for government ownership. Mining and oil production industries are in fact government owned in many countries, and there are examples where these state-owned enterprises have been efficiently run. These include Statoil in Norway, Petronas in Malaysia, Petrobras in Brazil, and PDVSA in República Bolivariana de Venezuela in the 1980s and 1990s. Nonetheless, cross-country studies have demonstrated that productivity generally improves significantly after privatization (Schmitz and Teixeira 2008; La Porta and Lopez de Silanes 1999; Chong and Lopez de Silanes 2005).[10] At the same time, private ownership of oil or mineral companies is likely to limit the scope of redistributional policies because private ownership is often accompanied by a lower fiscal take (government's share of the sector's profits). Hence, countries often face a trade-off. Privatized firms are more productive than nationalized enterprises in general, but privatization is often associated with increased inequality. This trade-off is linked to back-and-forth changes in ownership of the natural resource sector between the public and private sectors.

Nationalizations and privatizations of natural resource sectors are often cyclical phenomena and tend to come in waves across several countries at once. LAC countries are no exception. Chua (1995), in a comprehensive historical study of the privatization-nationalization cycle focused on Latin America and Southeast Asia, finds that despite their differences, the two regions share a tendency to move back and forth between nationalization and privatization. Compared with Southeast Asia (particularly Malaysia, Pakistan, and Thailand), the cycle started earlier in Latin America, with its longer post-independence history. In Latin America (most prominently in Argentina, Brazil, Chile, Mexico, Peru, and República Bolivariana de Venezuela), the first wave of privatization extended from the 1870s to the 1920s, a period of increased global integration. Partly in reaction to the Great Depression, nationalizations became frequent and extensive in the 1930s. A second tide of privatization occurred after World War II, only to be reversed under the populist regimes of the 1960s and 1970s. Two decades later, in the early 1990s, privatizations resurged on a massive scale.[11] Manzano and Monaldi (2008) report a trend toward renationalization in the last few years for a small group of mostly Latin America countries. Nationalizations in LAC have affected mainly resource extraction and utilities.

Several factors seem to affect the probability of nationalization

High commodity prices
Duncan (2006), analyzing the eight largest developing-country exporters of seven major minerals over 1960–2002, concludes that a high real price for minerals is a stronger predictor of state expropriation risk than are political or economic crises. Guriev, Kolotilin, and Sonin (2008), using panel data for 1960–2002, reach a similar conclusion for the oil industry. Manzano and Monaldi (2008) argue that

large rents and sunk costs make the oil industry very attractive for government expropriation when oil prices rise and the tax system is inadequate, in the sense of being regressive and lacking price-contingency clauses. The general implication of these studies is that contracting arrangements that give private companies a largely unrestrained ability to capture windfalls create incentives for nationalization when commodity prices are high.

More flexible arrangements can reduce the incentives for nationalization. This can occur through tax arrangements that allow the government to at least partially capture the upside when prices boom or, as is common, through renegotiation of contractual terms.

A case in point is Chile, where the private sector is currently (as of 2008) responsible for 74 percent of copper production. Chile introduced a royalty on the total profits of private mining companies in 2005. The private mining sector objected strenuously to the first bill by the government proposing this royalty tax, but opposition declined when a second bill was passed in 2005 (Navia 2010).[12] The bill had considerable popular support; a poll by CERC reported that 67 percent of Chilean adults supported a specific tax on mining activity. The imposition of the admittedly modest royalty does not appear to have worsened the investment climate. In a 2008–09 worldwide survey of mining investors, Chile ranked in the top five in the mineral potential index measuring the policy climate for mining exploration.[13] One explanation is that the low royalty might have reduced the political risk for the private sector by lessening pressures for a dramatic overhaul of the tax regime, or indeed a reversal of private control of the sector. Even though copper prices reached historically high levels during the latest boom, the sector is increasingly in the control of private (and foreign) hands. This recent experience, furthermore, stands in contrast to that of the sharp price hike of the 1970s, when copper was nationalized.

Entrenched inequality—especially when natural resource rents are perceived to benefit only a minority, and often a foreign minority at that
Chua (1995) shows that nationalizations in Latin America have been promoted against foreigners and

domestic residents perceived as unfairly privileged. This has been the case especially where private ownership and management of natural resource companies were seen to have worsened inequality. This is well illustrated in Bolivia, where the government's share of hydrocarbon production revenues fell significantly with privatization in the 1990s, while overall inequality rose substantially (figure 4.2). This, together with the proposed construction of a pipeline to Chile for future gas exports to the United States, led to increased opposition to what was perceived as exploitation of Bolivia's natural resources by foreign companies at the expense of the Bolivian people. This anti-elitist movement has played a significant role in the recent round of nationalizations in Latin America.

The quality of institutions and the degree of economic reliance on the commodity sector

Nationalization is more likely in countries with low human capital, undiversified production, and weak public institutions. Guriev, Kolotilin, and Sonin (2008) find that governments are more likely to nationalize when the quality of institutions (measured by indicators of institutionalized democracy and constraints on the executive) and human capital (measured by adult literacy) are deficient. Kobrin (1984) and Minor (1994) remark that countries experiencing mass expropriations tend to depend heavily on a few commodities. Several mechanisms may be at play. When public institutions are flawed, governments are more likely to violate contracts and ignore the rule of law, as reputational costs, domestic disapproval, and external sanctions are minimal. Moreover, when human capital is low and the economy poorly diversified, income and consumption tend to be more volatile under a privatized system. In addition, when the production structure is heavily concentrated in a few industries, such as natural resources, outside options for workers who are not well remunerated in those industries are quite limited.

This discussion suggests that the cyclical nature of the nationalization and privatization of natural resource industries appears to follow some self-reinforcing dynamics. Nationalizations are more likely when

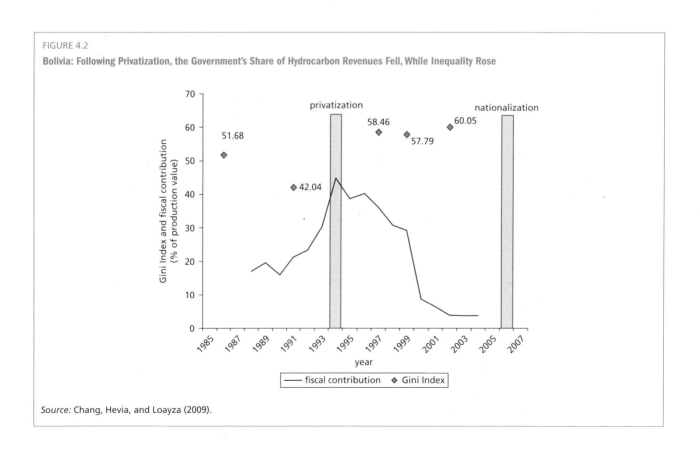

FIGURE 4.2

Bolivia: Following Privatization, the Government's Share of Hydrocarbon Revenues Fell, While Inequality Rose

Source: Chang, Hevia, and Loayza (2009).

commodity prices are high, inequality is extensive, and institutional quality is low. Furthermore, the incentive to nationalize rises where contracting and tax arrangements are inflexible, preventing governments from sharing in the upside of commodity price bonanzas. Reprivatization, by contrast, is more likely where commodity prices are low because of the greater efficiency in privately owned and managed natural resource exploitation. However, low commodity prices *and* the credibility lost during the previous nationalization combine to weaken the bargaining power of governments in reprivatization negotiations. Rather, the government may be induced to make greater concessions to attract private operators back to the natural resource sector. As a result, contractual arrangements for privatization may have to be fairly inflexible, excessively tying the hands of the government and not allowing it to partake in the upside. This, in turn, raises the probability of a renationalization during a future commodity bonanza, thus reinforcing the cycle. The cycle could be broken if the government could make a credible commitment not to renationalize, which would in turn allow it to negotiate better contractual terms.

Natural Resource Rents, Democracy, and Conflict

Studies of mineral-rich countries in the Middle East, Africa, and other regions have suggested that having abundant oil and other mineral resources inhibits democracy. Ross (2010) puts forward three potential channels. First, resource revenues may increase the repressive capacity of the state. Second, by discouraging taxation, natural resource revenues may diminish citizen pressures for greater state accountability, including through the adoption of representative institutions. Finally, the enclave character of much natural resource extraction may discourage broad modernizing changes, such as occupational diversity, that some scholars believe promote democracy. Ross (2010) finds econometric support for the second mechanism but not the first or third.

Yet, the claim that resources inhibit development or democracy does not explain important anomalies. For one, it fails to explain the coexistence of natural resource wealth and democracy in many of today's high-income countries and even in many resource-rich developing countries. In addition, some countries may be democracies not despite oil, but in part because of it. Karl (1987, 1997) argues that petroleum revenues were crucial in the emergence of democracy in República Bolivariana de Venezuela (see also Dunning 2008).

The theory of resource rents posits two conflicting effects on the political regime, implying that whether natural resource abundance is a "political curse" or not is essentially an empirical question. On the one hand, a commodity boom may strengthen the incentives to control the *distribution* of rents, diminishing the attractiveness of democracy to elites. This is the "direct," authoritarian effect of resource rents. On the other hand, a resource boom can vastly enhance the resources available to implement social policies, thereby reducing the threat of a nondemocratic *redistribution* of private income and increasing the attractiveness (or reducing the disutility) of democracy to elites. This is the "indirect," democratic effect of rents—indirect because it works through the effect of resource rents on the threat of redistribution. It is not obvious a priori that either effect would always dominate.

Even if natural resource wealth is found, on average, to have hindered democracy around the world, recent studies conclude that this does not appear to have been the case in LAC (Dunning 2008; Ross 2010; Haber and Menaldo 2009).[14] Evidence from LAC countries suggests that having natural resource wealth has not harmed—and may have helped—democracy. The examples of Ecuador and República Bolivariana de Venezuela—both of which became democracies in periods of high oil rents—are consistent with these studies.

Why is LAC an anomaly to the political curse of natural resources? One reason may be LAC's high inequality, which would make the threat of nondemocratic redistribution more worrisome for elites. The greater inequality that accompanies non-resource-derived income or wealth could raise the importance of the effect of resource rents in moderating redistributive conflict.

Second, state control of the resource sector might also help. Although state control may be associated with low productivity, it could enhance the state's ability to redistribute resource rents. If the democratizing influence of natural resources works through the distribution of rents, state control of mineral industries could have positive consequences for democracy. For example, in LAC countries where resources were controlled by a small private elite (for example, in Bolivia before the 1952 revolution; see Dunning 2008), the democratizing effects of mineral wealth seem to have been especially weak or nonexistent.

Third, compared with societies in which the redistribution of non-resource-derived income is not as important, mass political support for redistribution—a product of high inequality—might increase the pressure on elites, tipping the balance in favor of the democratizing effect of natural resource rents. Finally, the extent of resource dependence matters. Dunning (2009) suggests that countries where the total economy (rather than simply the government) is heavily dependent on natural resources are more likely to be authoritarian than are countries less dependent on natural resource production. LAC countries are far less dependent on natural resources than are many states in the Middle East or Africa.

Of course, the question goes well beyond that of a simple democratic-authoritarian dichotomy. Recently, some natural resource booms have been accompanied by a weakening of democracy in the region (less press freedom and less influence of the rule of law). This is a fruitful area for additional research.

Globally, oil is the commodity most linked with violent conflict. But again, LAC appears to be more resistant to these effects, with a lower occurrence of violent separatist and national conflicts than the rest of the world (table 4.1). Because Latin America has historically been impervious to separatist conflicts—with no wars of secession since the 19th century—rates of violent conflict have been lower in hydrocarbon producer countries there than elsewhere. That is not to say that natural resources—particularly hydrocarbons and minerals—are unrelated to conflicts in the region. Today, there are some 120 local conflicts concerning mining. But they are generally nonviolent disputes over land rights, labor practices, and environmental protection.

There are at least two possible explanations for this anomaly: the region's long history of sovereign statehood, which may have solidified national borders,

TABLE 4.1

Latin America Has Avoided Violent Conflicts

Conflict Onset Rates by Type, Latin America and Rest of the World

	Rest of world	Latin America
1960–1990		
Governmental wars	1.49*	2.39*
Separatist wars	1.15***	0.00***
All wars	2.64	2.39*
1991–2006		
Governmental wars	1.97**	0.69**
Separatist wars	2.53***	0.00***
All wars	4.5***	0.69***

Source: Ross (2010).
Note: The conflict onset rate represents the rate of emergence of new civil wars in the country-year sample. In the table, asterisks mark differences between the onset rate in Latin America and the rest of the world that are statistically significant.
*** $p < .01$, ** $p < .05$, * $p < .10$ in Pearson's chi-square test (rows 1 and 3) or a one-sided Fisher's exact test (rows 2, 4, 5, and 6). The tests are for values in rows (i.e., Rest of World vs. Latin America).

and the absence (until recently) of highly politicized ethnic cleavages. Perhaps separatism is a phenomenon that fades over time, a result of either causation (national boundaries become more widely accepted) or selection (less cohesive states fracture until the remaining units are more cohesive). Perhaps secessionist conflicts were worked out earlier in LAC history. (There were a large number of separatist wars in Latin America in the 19th century.) To be sure, petroleum extraction does seem to touch off the same kind of frustrations and protests in Latin America as elsewhere, trigger the same demands for distributive justice, and contribute to the same kinds of sabotage and extortion—most visibly in Bolivia, Colombia, Ecuador, and Mexico. Yet neither mineral wealth nor other circumstances have caused marginalized ethnic communities in any LAC country to fight for secession or independence. Overall, LAC countries seem to have found political arrangements and compromises that, despite high inequality, have managed to forestall the type of separatist struggles and violent conflict around natural resource wealth often observed in other developing regions.

Endnotes

1. For institutions, here we take the broad definition suggested by North (1990, p. 3): "Institutions are the rules of the game in a society or, more formally, are the humanly devised

constraints that shape human interaction. In consequence, they structure incentives in human exchange, whether political, social or economic." Institutions can be formal, consisting of rules, or informal, consisting of conventions and codes of behavior. Therefore, institutions as a concept encompass a broad range of political, economic, legal, and social arrangements.

2. For historical and econometric evidence that institutions have a first-order, independent effect on growth, see, for instance, Engerman and Sokoloff (1997, 2003); Hall and Jones (1999); Acemoglu, Johnson, and Robinson (2001, 2002, 2005); and Rodrik (2004). For an exploration of the role of institutions in Latin American and Caribbean development, see the World Bank's 1998 regional flagship for LAC, *Beyond the Washington Consensus: Institutions Matter*.

3. The Latin American institutions that emerged from the colonial exploitation of natural resources have been put forward as explaining the divergence in incomes from those of North America. This has been linked to differences in factor endowments that affected the incentives of colonial powers in shaping institutions (Engerman and Sokoloff 1997, 2003). Thus, the emergence of small holdings as the predominant form of agriculture in the northern United States and Canada, due in part to labor scarcity and soil conditions, led to enhanced equality and more democratic institutions, compared with societies in South America and the southern United States, where large-scale plantations led to inequality and weak institutions.

4. This thesis echoes the intuition arising from the "limited access order" framework of North et al. (2007). Under the authors' conjecture, to move from a system of limited access (for instance, one based on natural resource rents controlled by and for powerful elites) to one of open access, a society needs to cross a certain institutional quality threshold.

5. This distinction between resources that produce rents and those that do not parallels a distinction in the literature on natural resources and conflict between concentrated, lootable or "point-source" resources and geographically "diffuse" resources that are "non-lootable" by private actors (Le Billon 2001; Snyder 2001; Snyder and Bhavnani 2005; Isham et al. 2003).

6. Rather than directly emanating from competition for resource rents, the result in Baland and Francois's (2000) work is generated by import quotas. An economy can import or produce industrial goods domestically. The right to import industrial goods confers a rent that accrues to domestic rent seekers. The more individuals that produce the good, the cheaper it is, meaning that at some threshold, the import license becomes useless because it is cheaper to produce the good domestically.

7. A procyclical fiscal response to a commodity boom does not require, as a precondition, a particularly corrupt budget process or a weak set of institutions. As Talvi and Vegh (2005) point out, procyclical fiscal policy tends to be the rule rather than the exception throughout the world. In their model of fiscal policy, Talvi and Vegh introduce a political distortion that makes running budget surpluses costly for a government because of the pressure to increase spending. The greater the fluctuations in government revenues, the more important will be the political pressure to spend, as the budget surplus will deviate more from its average value. The authors suggest, then, that the procyclical fiscal policies seen in developing countries are due to the higher variability of the tax base relative to that of G-7 countries. In this framework, fiscal dependence on volatile commodity revenues would increase the variability of the tax base.

8. The background country studies are available on the project website at http://go.worldbank.org/55O3DOM6N0.

9. In the case of Chile, there is a proposal to replace *La Ley Reservada del Cobre*, which gives 10 percent of CODELCO sales to the military, with a transfer from general government resources that would allow the military a medium-term planning horizon for its expenditures.

10. Andres et al. (2008), in a study of infrastructure privatizations in LAC (water, electricity, and telecommunications utilities), also found "overall significant improvements in sector performance associated with private sector participation; with consistent improvements in efficiency and quality and reductions in workforce." They note, however, that within both the private and public sectors there was a great deal of variance, with the top public agencies performing as well as some private companies.

11. In keeping with Chua's findings are those of Kobrin (1984). Kobrin analyzed expropriations in 79 developing countries over the period 1960–79. He found that expropriations grew in the 1960s, peaked in the early 1970s, and declined afterward. Minor (1994) and Shafik (1996) extended Kobrin's study to include the period up to 1993. They found that, in the late 1980s and early 1990s, as many as 95 countries around the world experienced extensive privatization processes.

12. The bill of 2005 was also no doubt better received by mining companies because of the concessions in terms of accelerated depreciation that the Lagos administration made for private companies, which delayed the paying of the tax.

13. *Source:* Fraser Institute's Annual Survey of Mining Companies 2008–2009.

14. In particular, Haber and Menaldo (2009) find a positive relationship between natural resources and democracy in a longer time series for Latin America when the latter variable is measured in levels. However, when democracy is first-differenced by year, and when possible nonstationarities are addressed, the authors find no relationship, on average, between natural resources and the political regime. Within LAC, then, this study does not support the claim that oil has hindered democracy.

CHAPTER 5

Managing Commodity Price Volatility

Key messages: Commodity price shocks have strong ripple effects on both general economic activity and fiscal revenues. This is exacerbated by governments' reliance on commodity-based revenue, a result of both Dutch disease effects and neglect of other, less volatile forms of taxation. The reliance on commodity revenues has been growing in LAC. Rapidly increasing commodity revenues during booms have fueled fiscal expansions, with spending in some cases rising more than revenues. This pattern held for the last boom in LAC, with the notable exceptions of Bolivia and Chile.

To deal with revenue instability—and wealth preservation over the long term—countries have used stabilization and sovereign wealth funds, fiscal rules, and fiscal responsibility legislation with mixed success. These measures have often been abandoned when public pressure built to spend the proceeds of the boom period, as occurred in Ecuador and República Bolivariana de Venezuela in the recent cycle. Commodity price shocks are transmitted to the exchange rate. Adjustment of the real exchange is slower with a less flexible exchange rate regime, because the adjustment takes place through a change in the general price level over time, rather than through a quick shift in the nominal exchange rate. Of course, more flexible regimes may be subject to greater real exchange rate volatility in the face of volatile terms of trade. The burden of such volatility may be lowered through the use of a well-designed natural resource stabilization or long-term savings funds.

Mismanagement of the short-run volatility associated with commodity dependence may slow long-term growth through many channels (see chapter 3). Three channels are particularly important to LAC countries: volatility of export income (accentuated by export concentration), instability of fiscal spending (particularly public investments in health, education, and infrastructure), and systematic undersaving (or overconsumption) of natural resource revenues. These channels of transmission can result in volatility in short-run aggregate demand and output and in wealth depletion, slowing growth in the long run. Thus, these adverse effects on growth materialize largely to the extent that governments fail to save enough from commodity income or to dampen the transmission to the domestic economy of the volatility inherent in commodities.

This section focuses on the challenges that commodity price volatility poses for macroeconomic policy, particularly fiscal stabilization policy but also exchange rate policy. Undersaving of natural resource income is briefly examined in the analysis of the fiscal implications. We begin the discussion by considering the relationship between export shocks and shocks to real economic output.

Commodity Price Volatility, Export Concentration, and Output Volatility Are Linked

Commodity-exporting countries, whether rich, middle-income, or poor, are exposed to commodity price volatility. But its impact on aggregate demand, saving and investment, and output rises with the degree of export concentration. This is a key dimension that differentiates high-income, natural resource–rich countries from the commodity-exporting countries in LAC: high-income countries have much less export concentration (see figure 2.3). While the "risk" (the probability of commodity price changes) is the same for both classes of countries, the "value at risk" (the degree of dependence of total export income on commodity exports) is substantially lower for the high-income commodity exporters.

Through pronounced Dutch disease–type effects of natural resource discoveries and export booms, commodity abundance may lead to concentrated (or undiversified) export baskets. Without price volatility, export concentration might not be inconsistent with maximizing social welfare, since it may reflect strong comparative advantage. But volatility can reduce welfare by undercutting long-term growth. Although the direct connections between commodity price volatility and long-run growth are difficult to establish empirically, econometric work has found a strong positive association between export concentration and volatility in terms of trade and output growth (Lederman and Xu 2009). Moreover, the positive link between commodity price volatility and output variability appears to be nonlinear: larger price shocks result in disproportionately larger short-run fluctuations in output relative to smaller shocks (Camacho and Pérez 2010).

Furthermore, the effects of commodity price fluctuations on growth rate stability seem to be asymmetric and to vary with the cyclical state of the economy (Camacho and Pérez 2010). Positive price shocks have larger effects during recessions than during booms, while negative shocks have a greater effect in good than in bad times. In line with the value at risk reasoning, countries with high shares of commodity exports in total exports are more strongly affected by commodity price changes. Of course, the effect on output volatility of a one-time commodity price shock dies out over time, as illustrated for Colombia in figure 5.1.

These findings underscore the importance of export diversification for immunizing natural resource–abundant countries against the adverse effects of

commodity price volatility. But commodity-rich countries tend to experience Dutch disease effects that discourage diversification into noncommodity exports. These effects can be reduced by insulating the domestic economy from shocks to exports. Much of the burden of creating such a shock absorber falls on macroeconomic policy, to which we now turn.

Hydrocarbon and Mining Provide a Substantial—and Growing—Share of Fiscal Revenues in the Region

A heavy reliance on commodities for fiscal revenues contributes to the volatility of revenues and procyclicality in budget execution in LAC. As noted in the literature on the procyclicality of fiscal policy in the region (Gavin and Perotti 1997), this has involved burgeoning debt levels and inefficient public spending during booms, with deleterious economic effects. Countries expand spending during commodity price booms, unleashing strong real exchange rate appreciation, and are then forced to cut spending and allow sharp devaluations of the real exchange rate during busts. In what follows, we discuss the revenue response to the recent commodity price bonanza and examine the impact on fiscal expenditures in commodity-dependent LAC economies.

The large share of fiscal revenues derived from commodities in LAC commodity-rich countries exacerbates the volatility of fiscal revenues. Worse, the share of revenues derived from commodities appears to be rising in mineral- and hydrocarbon-rich LAC countries. Natural resource revenues are much more volatile than other revenues (figure 5.2). LAC countries rely more on this volatile source of revenues for their tax base than do high-income commodity producers. Although LAC fiscal revenues from commodities as a share of GDP were similar to those in Canada and Norway in 2004, a quarter of the revenue was sourced from commodity production and export in LAC compared with 2.5 percent in Canada and 14.6 percent in Norway, because high-income commodity producers collect more tax revenues from other sources. The overreliance on commodity revenues creates a large challenge for LAC governments in moderating the impact of commodity revenue cycles on the economy.

FIGURE 5.1

The Impulse Response Function to a Commodity Price Shock in Colombia

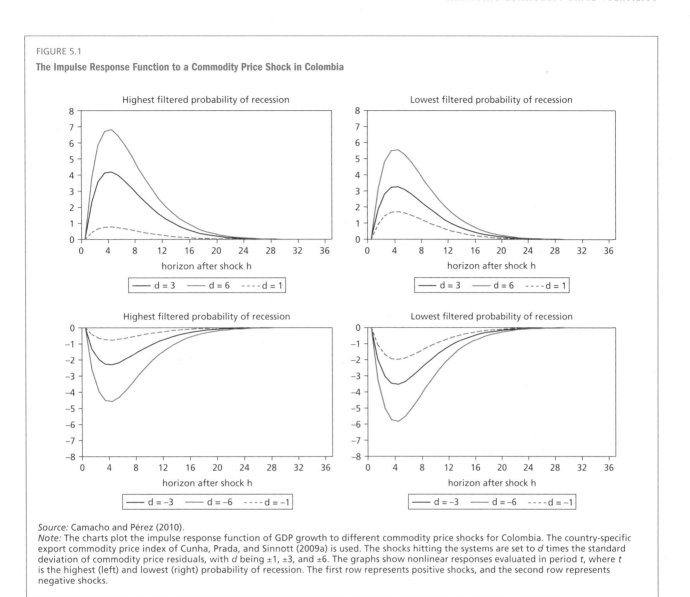

Source: Camacho and Pérez (2010).
Note: The charts plot the impulse response function of GDP growth to different commodity price shocks for Colombia. The country-specific export commodity price index of Cunha, Prada, and Sinnott (2009a) is used. The shocks hitting the systems are set to d times the standard deviation of commodity price residuals, with d being ±1, ±3, and ±6. The graphs show nonlinear responses evaluated in period t, where t is the highest (left) and lowest (right) probability of recession. The first row represents positive shocks, and the second row represents negative shocks.

High hydrocarbon rents may reduce other forms of taxation

Making matters worse, the reliance on natural resources may dampen other revenue generation efforts, exacerbating the concentration and volatility of fiscal revenue. Taxing mineral resources makes life easier for politicians—they can dole out resources without having to tax most residents and firms. Because the ready availability of commodity-based fiscal income can raise the political cost of collecting traditional taxes, politicians may opt to reduce traditional tax rates as a way of distributing rents (Dunning 2009). Thus, a high dependence on commodities can constitute a self-reinforcing equilibrium.

There is empirical evidence for this effect and for its leading to greater volatility in overall revenues. Bornhorst, Gupta, and Thornton (2009), in a study of 30 hydrocarbon-producing countries—including Ecuador, Mexico, Trinidad and Tobago, and República Bolivariana de Venezuela—during 1992–2005, find that countries that receive large revenues from hydrocarbons raise less revenue from other domestic taxes. A cross-country analysis by Knack (2008) provides evidence that tax effort—as measured by the efficiency of revenue mobilization rating from the World Bank's Country Policy and Institutional Assessments—is lower for large hydrocarbon exporters. And case study evidence strongly suggests that resource booms have eroded the

FIGURE 5.2

Volatility of Commodity Revenue Is Much Higher Than That from Other Sources

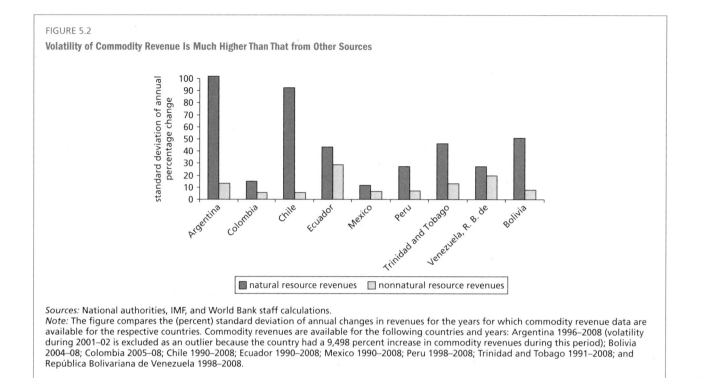

Sources: National authorities, IMF, and World Bank staff calculations.
Note: The figure compares the (percent) standard deviation of annual changes in revenues for the years for which commodity revenue data are available for the respective countries. Commodity revenues are available for the following countries and years: Argentina 1996–2008 (volatility during 2001–02 is excluded as an outlier because the country had a 9,498 percent increase in commodity revenues during this period); Bolivia 2004–08; Colombia 2005–08; Chile 1990–2008; Ecuador 1990–2008; Mexico 1990–2008; Peru 1998–2008; Trinidad and Tobago 1991–2008; and República Bolivariana de Venezuela 1998–2008.

non-resource-derived tax base in Latin America and elsewhere (Soifer 2006; Dunning 2008).

The fiscal response to the recent boom has been uneven

Fiscal positions have responded more strongly to positive commodity shocks in LAC than in high-income exporters (Medina 2010). This remained the case during the recent commodity price boom for many LAC commodity producers, with the exception of Chile, which behaved similarly to high-income countries. Real primary expenditures rose in all the fiscally dependent commodity countries during the boom.[1] Use of the increased fiscal revenues to fund primary spending rose gradually, with a slower response in the early years of the boom (figure 5.3). However, there was considerable variability. Saving out of the commodity windfall was greater in Bolivia and Chile, where primary expenditures grew substantially more slowly than total revenues and with primary expenditure growth about equal to the contribution of noncommodity revenues to total revenue growth. By contrast, in Colombia, Ecuador, Peru, Trinidad and Tobago, and República Bolivariana de Venezuela, primary expenditures grew somewhat

faster than total revenue, particularly in the second half of the boom.[2] For these oil producers, spending grew much faster than did the contribution of non-commodity revenues to overall revenue growth.

The IMF (2009a) finds a similar pattern across countries when comparing the growth of primary spending to that of trend GDP. Primary expenditures increased much more than trend GDP growth during the height of the boom years in the group of LAC countries categorized as "other commodity exporting countries" (Argentina, Bolivia, Ecuador, Paraguay, Suriname, Trinidad and Tobago, and República Bolivariana de Venezuela). For these countries, this implies a strong fiscal response in the boom years.

Much of the spending favored public investment. Thus, the pattern Gelb (1990) observed during the 1974–78 oil price shock—faster growth in public investment than in other expenditures for six oil exporters—obtained again in the recent boom, as growth in capital spending outpaced that for current spending. LAC capital budgets grew fast but from a low base. And growth in current expenditures was tilted in favor of large increases in subsidies and transfers. Some countries, including Chile and República Bolivariana de Venezuela, used part of the proceeds to fund

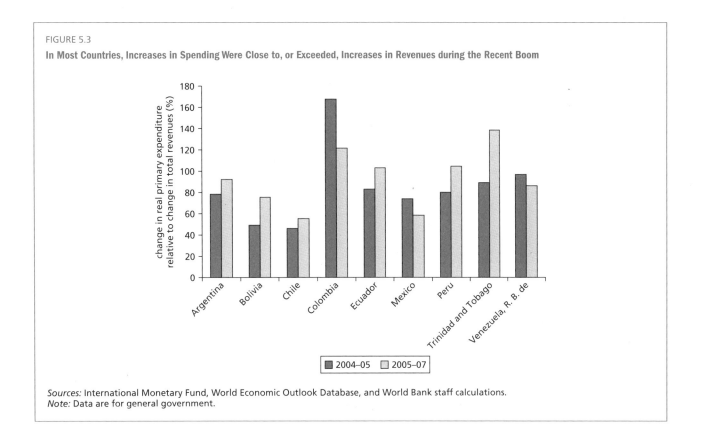

FIGURE 5.3

In Most Countries, Increases in Spending Were Close to, or Exceeded, Increases in Revenues during the Recent Boom

Sources: International Monetary Fund, World Economic Outlook Database, and World Bank staff calculations.
Note: Data are for general government.

increases in health, education, social housing, and social protection programs, albeit with very different styles of fiscal management and intertemporal fiscal prudence.

Many LAC commodity producers entered the global crisis—in particular the economic downturn that triggered the collapse of Lehman Brothers in September 2008—with much stronger fiscal positions and lower public sector debt burdens than during previous crises. Public sector balances had been improving in LAC over the past decade or so. Calderon and Fajnzylber (2009) provide econometric evidence that LAC fiscal processes have become more viable even if they remain procyclical. The pre-crisis commodity price boom was not associated with the large increases in indebtedness experienced in the past. Rather, many countries used the windfall to reduce public-sector debt and increase foreign reserves.

However, the vulnerability to a decline in commodity prices has increased among LAC mineral and oil producers, with the exceptions of Chile and Peru, as evidenced by their fiscal position excluding commodity-related revenues. On average, the noncommodity primary balance of large (relative to total

exports) oil exporters declined significantly each year over 2005–08, whereas that of other commodity-dependent countries improved. Oil-reliant economies such as Ecuador, Mexico, Trinidad and Tobago, and República Bolivariana de Venezuela have developed large non-oil fiscal deficits, whereas the mineral producers—Chile and Peru—managed to run noncommodity primary surpluses by the end of the period (figure 5.4).

As commodity exporters emerged from the commodity boom, they evidenced a large divergence in the fiscal space for countercyclical fiscal policy. Chile had built up large fiscal resources in its stabilization fund, Fondo de Estabilizacion Economica y Social (Chilean Economic and Social Stabilization Fund), during the pre-crisis copper boom that allowed the country to follow an ambitious countercyclical agenda once the downturn began. Chile had accumulated US$20 billion, equivalent to about 12 percent of GDP, in its stabilization fund by the end of 2008. About half the reserves were used to fund the initial countercyclical fiscal package, permitting Chile to finance a substantial part of a 14.5 percent increase in public spending in real terms (IMF 2009b).

FIGURE 5.4

Fiscal Positions of LAC Commodity Exporters over the Recent Boom

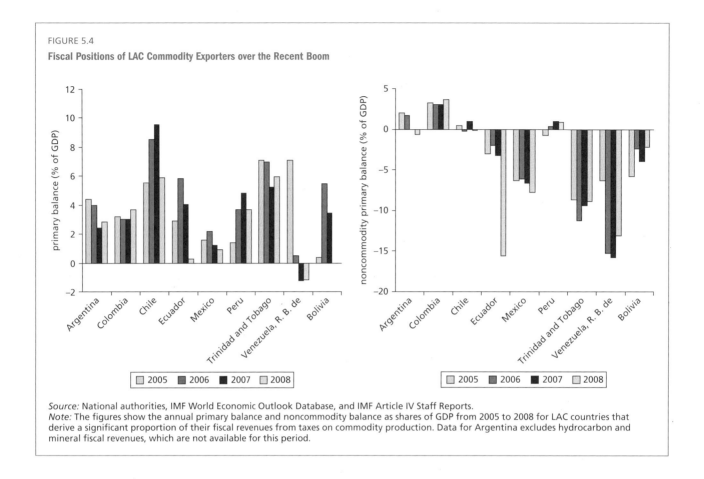

Source: National authorities, IMF World Economic Outlook Database, and IMF Article IV Staff Reports.
Note: The figures show the annual primary balance and noncommodity balance as shares of GDP from 2005 to 2008 for LAC countries that derive a significant proportion of their fiscal revenues from taxes on commodity production. Data for Argentina excludes hydrocarbon and mineral fiscal revenues, which are not available for this period.

Bolivia, Peru, and to a lesser extent Mexico were also able to accumulate fiscal savings out of the pre-crisis windfalls and use them—in different degrees—to fund countercyclical spending. By contrast, Ecuador and República Bolivariana de Venezuela did not manage to accumulate large savings from the pre-crisis windfall and so had to reduce primary expenditures in 2009 because of the decline in commodity revenues in the second half of 2008 and the first quarter of 2009 (IMF 2009a).

Countries have had mixed experience using different fiscal instruments to manage volatility

Many natural resource (fiscally)–dependent countries in LAC and around the world have established fiscal rules, natural resource stabilization funds, and fiscal responsibility legislation to deal with volatile fiscal rents from natural resources.[3] These mainly apply to hydrocarbons and minerals, given that export taxes on agricultural commodities have tended to wane, and their relative

importance in fiscal revenues has tended to fall. Some governments in LAC's resource-rich countries (e.g., Bolivia, Peru) have self-insured by simply accumulating regular deposits in their central banks. To make this sort of prudency a reality, some countries have moreover used a conservative—that is, lower-than-expected—commodity price as a reference to formulate the budget. Of course, the less formal stabilization-oriented fiscal-saving mechanisms face greater risks of being breached. There are frequent examples where commodity fiscal revenues in excess of those forecast by the budget have been consumed via off-budget spending driven by clientelist considerations.

Other countries have used more formal arrangements. Formal stabilization funds, for example, have been used in Chile and Mexico to reduce the impact of volatile prices on fiscal spending. In practice, these fiscal rules and funds conflate multiple objectives, beyond that of smoothing fiscal spending in the face of volatile and unpredictable natural resource revenues across the cycle (a basic purpose, for instance, of the Chilean Economic and Social Stabilization Fund, Fees). Other objectives, some of which will be discussed below, include the equitable distribution across generations of the natural resource income (a central objective, for instance, of Norway's Government Pension Fund); the protection of the poor and other vulnerable groups in times of cyclical downturns (see Engel, Nielsen, and Valdés 2010, who find that the welfare gains of such a social policy fiscal rule are particularly high where there is greater income inequality); the mitigation of real exchange rate appreciation (one rationale behind the fact that Chile's two sovereign wealth funds are invested abroad); and asset diversification (an explicit motive of Trinidad and Tobago's Heritage and Stabilization Fund, HSF). Additionally, fiscal rules and dedicated funds typically aim at increasing transparency and accountability in the spending of natural resource revenues, in line, for instance, with the Extractive Industries Transparency Initiative (EITI).

The decision on the optimal use of natural resource rents is then quite complex,[4] and the institutional mechanisms to save resources reflect this intricacy, often combining a number of diverse aims. Most natural resource funds are based on twin policy objectives of stabilization and saving. For example, the interest and dividends from Norway's sovereign wealth fund are used to balance the structural, non-oil deficit in bad times, whereas the principal can only be used to cover future pension liabilities. The key point is that a long-term saving function in fiscal policy is essential to adequately address the challenges posed by nonrenewable natural resources. The typical policy instrument in this regard is the so-called sovereign wealth fund. The accumulation of long-term savings out of windfall rents in this sort of fund is typically subject to special rules and governance arrangements, as well as to different investment criteria compared to stabilization-oriented funds. The latter tend to be invested in foreign securities that are safe and highly liquid, whereas the former tend to be invested within a long-term horizon in a diversified portfolio, where less liquid and riskier assets have a nontrivial weight.

Of the five countries that began the recent boom in 2002 with a stabilization fund or other fiscal

arrangements to manage windfall hydrocarbon or mineral revenues, only two delivered results in terms of significant windfall savings at the end of the boom. These were Chile's FEES and Trinidad and Tobago's HSF. Both Chile's and Trinidad and Tobago's funds endured, with each country accumulating savings equivalent to 12 percent of GDP by the end of 2008. Ecuador and República Bolivariana de Venezuela dispensed with their arrangements. Ecuador breached its fiscal deficit and spending rules, which were unable to survive political and social pressures, ultimately leading to a revision of the fiscal responsibility law in 2005 in favor of higher spending, and to the law's elimination in 2008. República Bolivariana de Venezuela stopped contributions to its Macroeconomic Stabilization Fund (Fondo de Estabilización Macroeconómica, FEM) soon after the fund's inception in 2003. In fact, República Bolivariana de Venezuela chose to spend much of its increased oil revenues off budget. Although for Mexico, the fiscal responsibility framework lasted and generated consistent primary surpluses during the boom period, it did not result in sufficient savings to finance a strong countercyclical package. Accumulation in oil-savings funds was capped at 1.5 percent of GDP (IMF 2010a).

Price Volatility Also Is a Problem at the Household Level, Especially for Food and Fuels

Although the focus of this section is on more aggregate effects on the economy, government, and society as a whole, commodity price volatility is also a problem for households in which a significant share of income either is spent on commodities or comes from commodity production, whether through direct reliance on production and sales or through the labor market. Commodity price shocks can also impact the poor and vulnerable through reduced fiscal space that limits social spending in times of need. To cope with price risks within the constraints they face, households may follow ex ante strategies (e.g., crop diversification, diversification of income-generating activities, precautionary savings to smooth consumption)[5] and ex post strategies (e.g., short-term consumption credit and informal help or compensation arrangements between members of a group or village) (see Deaton 1991;

Alderman and Paxson 1992; Dercon 2004). Of course, the choice of low-risk activities to cope with price shocks may involve a trade-off in the form of lower average return. The evidence suggests that despite all the smoothing strategies adopted voluntarily by households, substantial residual consumption risk remains (Jalan and Ravallion 1999).

While social spending should be countercyclical, historically it has tended to be either acyclical or procyclical (although possibly with some reversal of this tendency in the current global downturn). This has typically reflected the inability of countries to borrow at reasonable costs in bad times, so that when the fiscal space shrinks, social spending has as well. In the latest global crisis, however, LAC countries were better able to respond to the external shock (which also included a temporary but major fall in commodity prices), and social spending was maintained and even increased in several countries. The ability of the fiscal process to help cushion the shock in the latest crisis is a clear sign that the region has made significant strides toward improving its macroeconomic fundamentals, as emphasized in recent (biannual) reports of the World Bank for the Latin American region. The need to smooth social spending across time and possibly make it countercyclical calls for delaying some of the spending until "bad times." This likely requires some special provisions in the commodity-related macro-stabilization funds, complemented by a structure of effective social safety nets that enables the expansion of social assistance when a crisis hits.

Commodity price shocks, especially those affecting socially sensitive goods such as internationally tradable foods and fuels, tend to have complex distributional implications not just in countries that are importers of such commodities, but even in those that are net exporters. In the latter case, although an increase in international commodity prices benefits the country as a whole, the pass-through of the international price rise to the domestic prices can raise social tensions because some groups in society lose while others gain. This was illustrated clearly in Argentina during the recent spike (2007–08) in the international prices of foods and fuels, where, faced with protests from the urban poor and middle classes, the authorities introduced domestic price controls and limits on exports

of commodities that are also significantly consumed at home. One lesson is that in the absence of a permanent structure of well-functioning social safety nets, the optimal policy (allow domestic prices to reflect international prices and use fiscal transfer to compensate the losers) is politically difficult to implement.

Exchange Rate Policy

The volatile nature of revenue flows from commodities also has implications for exchange rate policy. Of course, the burden of such volatility on the exchange rate will be higher in the absence of the kind of well-designed, stabilization-oriented, and long-term-saving-oriented funds discussed earlier. The exchange rate regime that can best deal with such residual volatility is not independent of the specific conditions of the country.

With any exchange rate regime, however, a shock to the terms of trade will require, in equilibrium, a change in the real exchange rate (defined as the relative price of tradables to nontradables)—a real devaluation in the case of a negative shock, or a real appreciation in the case of a positive one. With a floating exchange rate, this will be accomplished through a change in the nominal rate, which can happen quite quickly. With a fixed rate, the adjustment must be accomplished through a change in domestic prices: that is, inflation for a real depreciation and deflation for a real appreciation. This process may take substantially longer than an adjustment in a flexible rate. Of course, between floating and pure fixed, there exist a wide range of intermediate regimes, either de jure or de facto. Few countries maintain pure floats; among the countries with even the most flexible regimes, intervention in LAC has been common during the recent commodity price cycle (Kiguel and Okseniuk 2010).

Although it is a matter of heated debate, a strong case can be made that a flexible exchange rate regime is more suited to dealing with commodity price volatility in countries that have a relatively large nontradable sector, experience real shocks that are asymmetric to those in their main trading partners, and are significantly integrated within international financial markets. A key reason behind this argument is that, in such countries, the equilibrium real exchange rate will itself tend to be volatile, responding to volatile terms of trade. By contrast, a fixed exchange rate regime might be a better option for commodity-exporting countries that are very open, have a relatively small nontradable sector, and experience shocks that are symmetric to those in their main trading partners (i.e., countries that meet "optimal currency area" conditions). This, again, is in part because, in the latter type of countries, the equilibrium real exchange rate would not need to adjust significantly in response to terms-of-trade shocks. An important consequence of this distinction is that countries in the first group that nonetheless adhere to hard pegs or less flexible exchange rate regimes need to compensate by greater flexibility in nominal wages and fiscal policy in order to achieve adjustments in the real exchange rate without excessive adjustments in quantities (output, employment), particularly during periods of terms-of-trade deterioration.

To be sure, countries do not generally choose their exchange rate regimes only in light of whether they are commodity exporters or not, and many other factors, including the degree of trade and financial openness as well as institutional considerations, play a role. In fact, there has been a general trend toward increased

exchange rate flexibility over the last 30 years in LAC. This process has intensified since the foreign exchange crises that hit many emerging-market countries in the late 1990s, and since the collapse of the currency board in Argentina in 2002.

The advantages and disadvantages of different exchange rate regimes in the context of the most recent commodity price cycle (with a focus on the 2004–09 period) were empirically assessed by Kiguel and Okseniuk (2010) in a paper prepared for this report. The authors compare the adjustment paths of the real exchange rates for three groups of LAC countries, confirming that those with flexible rate regimes adjusted most quickly, those with fixed rates the most slowly, and the intermediate regimes in the middle (figure 5.5).

On one hand, greater exchange rate flexibility implied less inflation during the commodity price boom years and better capacity to run countercyclical monetary policy in the downturn. Countries with floating exchange rate systems were thus somewhat more successful in limiting the impact of the "agflation" phenomenon during 2007 and 2008. The main reason is that they partially compensated for the increase in

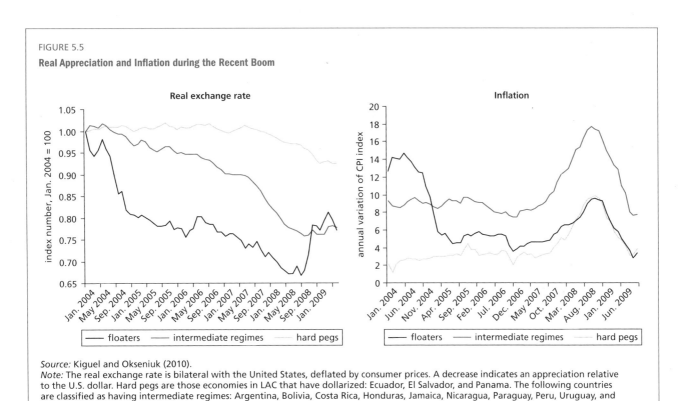

FIGURE 5.5

Real Appreciation and Inflation during the Recent Boom

Source: Kiguel and Okseniuk (2010).
Note: The real exchange rate is bilateral with the United States, deflated by consumer prices. A decrease indicates an appreciation relative to the U.S. dollar. Hard pegs are those economies in LAC that have dollarized: Ecuador, El Salvador, and Panama. The following countries are classified as having intermediate regimes: Argentina, Bolivia, Costa Rica, Honduras, Jamaica, Nicaragua, Paraguay, Peru, Uruguay, and República Bolivariana de Venezuela. The floaters consist of Brazil, Chile, Colombia, the Dominican Republic, Guatemala, and Mexico.

international prices of food and energy through the nominal appreciation of their currencies. During the downturn in prices that started in mid-2008, the floaters had a faster adjustment in the real exchange rate (although there was also some overshooting), and they were able to sharply reduce nominal interest rates as part of the stimulus packages to compensate the adverse external shocks. In addition, the countries that had less flexible regimes in general (including countries that are formally dollarized or have hard pegs) had to increase interest rates to defend parity and to limit capital outflows. When a real depreciation was required in the bust phase of the cycle, this had to be accomplished through a politically difficult reduction in domestic prices and wages.

On the other hand, a disadvantage of flexible regimes is their greater real exchange rate volatility (as is clear from figure 5.5). This brings with it difficulties when deciding to intervene to mitigate the impact of temporary exchange rate volatility on the noncommodity export sectors. For larger countries with more substantial nontradable sectors, this may present a particularly thorny problem. Inappropriate intervention may lead to a sharp short-run overshooting of the exchange rate relative to fundamental values. Intervention is also associated with the problem of domestic liquidity management of growing foreign exchange reserves due to sterilization when commodity prices are booming.

For countries with floating regimes, the recent performance of inflation-targeting countries has shown advantages in comparison with fixed exchange rate regimes for commodity producers. The adoption of an inflation anchor in many of the countries in the region has brought credibility and transparency to monetary policy frameworks. The most popular regime has been to target the consumer price index (CPI). However, Frankel (2009), in a paper prepared for this report, argues that events of the past few years, particularly the global financial crisis of 2007–09, may have somewhat strained inflation-targeting regimes. In particular, during this period, the price shock was a supply one, and inflation targeting is admittedly best suited to control inflation pressures arising from excess aggregate demand (relative to potential output). Hence, the authorities in inflation-targeting countries in LAC had to focus not solely on the CPI, but also on the exchange rate and the prices of agricultural and mineral products, as well as on their second-round effects on inflation expectations.[6] This is problematic partly because of regime credibility issues but also because of the fact that commodity prices are not given a weight in the CPI that their volatility warrants. The solution to this problem, however, is not simple, particularly for commodity-dependent countries. Frankel (2009) argues that, with this type of inflation targeting, countries would achieve lower domestic price volatility by targeting the producer price index instead of the CPI, as the former takes into account much better the most volatile prices of a country's exports or a more comprehensive group of a country's exports (box 5.1).

BOX 5.1.

Potential Anchors for Monetary Policy for Commodity Producers and Consumers

Fixed and floating exchange rates each have their advantages. However, econometric attempts to discern what sort of regime delivers the best economic performance across countries—fixed, floating, or intermediate—have not been successful. The answer depends on the circumstances of the country in question. The CPI is the most common choice of the possible price indexes that a central bank could target. The CPI is indeed the natural candidate to be the measure of the inflation objective for the long term. But it may not be the best choice for an intermediate target on an annual basis. There is a case to be made for instead targeting either the producer price index (PPI) or an export price index. The latter idea is a moderate version of a more exotic monetary regime, proposed by Frankel and Saiki (2002) and Frankel (2003), called Peg the Export Price (PEP). Frankel (2009) examines possible nominal variables as candidates to be anchor for monetary policy. Three candidates are exchange rate pegs, to the dollar, euro, and SDR; one candidate is orthodox inflation targeting; and two candidates represent proposals where

(Box continues on next page)

BOX 5.1

(continued)

prices of exports are given substantial weight and prices of imports are not: PEP and PPI. The selling point of these production-based indexes is that each could accommodate shocks in terms of trade.

The proposed PEP regime targets the leading commodity of a country in question. The proposal is to fix the price of that commodity in terms of domestic currency. For example, Bolivia would peg its currency to natural gas; Chile would peg to copper; Ecuador, Trinidad and Tobago, and the República Bolivariana de Venezuela would peg to oil; Jamaica would peg to aluminum; the Dominican Republic would peg to sugar; Central American coffee producers would peg to coffee; and Argentina would peg to soybeans. An advantage of the PEP anchor is that it results in automatic adjustments in the face of fluctuations in the prices of the countries' exports on world markets. When the dollar price of exports rises (or falls), then the currency appreciates (or depreciates) in terms of dollars. Such accommodation of terms-of-trade shocks is precisely what is wanted. The side effect of using PEP is that it would destabilize the local-currency price of other tradable goods. If agricultural or mineral

commodities constitute virtually all of exports, then this may not be an issue; however, for most countries in LAC, no single commodity constitutes more than half of exports. Exports are dominated by agricultural and mineral commodities, but it is a diversified basket of commodities. A more flexible and broad-ranging variant of the commodity price peg would take export diversification into account, aiming to stabilize a more comprehensive index of export prices in terms of the local currency. Finally, a more moderate version is to target the producer price index (PPI), which includes a substantial commodity component.

Frankel (2009) shows a counterfactual analysis of alternative monetary regimes using the different nominal targets to simulate their ability to minimize both variability in the real price of commodity exports and variability in the real price of other traded goods. Frankel follows the logic that stabilizing the relative price of commodity exports is not much of an accomplishment if it comes at the expense of a corresponding destabilization of the relative price of other traded goods. The study focuses on a set of countries in LAC and compares the historical paths of

Standard Deviation of Level of Real Prices

	Real Prices						
	Historical regime	Dollar peg	SDR peg	Euro peg	Comm. peg	CPI target	PPI target
ARG	0.661	0.491	0.503	0.486	0.241	0.756	0.679
BOL	0.538	0.443	0.457	0.486	0.138	0.488	0.448
BRA	0.522	0.456	0.442	0.426	0.187	—	—
CHL	0.510	0.485	0.489	0.470	0.298	0.840	0.696
COL	0.456	0.485	0.482	0.490	0.000	1.123	0.974
CRI	0.420	0.368	0.383	0.385	0.242	—	—
ECU	0.456	0.485	0.482	0.490	0.000	—	—
GTM	0.510	0.588	0.600	0.585	0.383	—	—
GUY	0.922	0.581	0.579	0.557	0.383	—	—
HND	0.533	0.588	0.600	0.585	0.383	—	—
JAM	0.338	0.383	0.401	0.403	0.212	0.870	0.483
MEX	0.479	0.485	0.482	0.490	0.000	0.975	1.030
NIC	0.511	0.588	0.600	0.585	0.339	—	—
PAN	0.312	0.368	0.383	0.385	0.206	—	—
PER	0.444	0.485	0.489	0.470	0.171	0.420	0.429
PRY	0.413	0.455	0.475	0.466	0.312	0.743	0.716
SLV	0.750	0.588	0.600	0.585	0.383	—	—
TTO	0.383	0.443	0.457	0.486	0.179	—	—
URY	0.504	0.455	0.475	0.466	0.312	0.793	0.525
VEN	0.429	0.485	0.482	0.490	0.000	—	—

Source: Frankel (2009).
Note: The figures show the average of the export price standard deviation and import price standard deviation.

(Box continues on next page)

BOX 5.1

(continued)

prices under the actual monetary regime with what would have happened under the other possible regimes. The analysis presumes that for commodity-producing countries such as those in LAC, a highly volatile terms-of-trade regime is perhaps the most important issue to be addressed by currency policy.

Based on Frankel's simulations, all nominal anchors (pegs) deliver greater overall nominal price stability than the inflationary historical monetary regimes actually followed by LAC countries, and the PEP proposal ("Comm peg" column) is found to be the best anchor for reducing relative price variability. Also, the PEP and PPI alternative inflation targeting anchors dominate a policy targeting the CPI with respect to terms-of-trade shocks. The PEP and PPI have the desirable property that the currency appreciates (or depreciates) when prices for exports go up (or down) on world markets; the CPI does not have that property. In addition, if inflation targeting is interpreted strictly as a commitment to the CPI, then it has the undesirable property that the currency appreciates (or depreciates) when the prices of imports go up (or down)

on world markets; PEP and PPI targeting do not have this undesirable property.

An interesting finding is the comparison of a CPI target and a PPI target as alternative interpretations of inflation targets. The results show that the PPI target generally delivers more stability in the prices of traded goods, especially the export commodity. This is a natural consequence of the larger weight on commodity exports in the PPI than in the CPI. Perhaps surprisingly, both the CPI target and the PPI target deliver more relative price variability than any of the three exchange rate pegs (dollar, euro, and SDR). Frankel suggests that more research is needed to clarify this. Estimates are made for the weights that the countries' CPI and PPI place on each of three sectors: nontradable goods, the leading commodity export, and other tradables. Thus, it may be necessary to see if the estimation of these weights and the price series can be improved and the comparison made more realistic by allowing the CPI and PPI to fall within a range rather than requiring the central bank to hit a target precisely.

Source: Frankel (2009).

This proposal is likely to be unpalatable to central banks, however, not least because the headline inflation, as measured by the CPI, remains as the most visible and relevant price variable to societies.

Endnotes

1. The period 2005–07 is used to examine the response to the boom, given that reliable cross-country fiscal data are available only on an annual basis and that commodity prices took a nosedive in the second half of 2008.

2. The expenditure data for República Bolivariana de Venezuela shown in figure 5.3 do not reflect the true magnitude of spending during the recent boom. Much of the spending was carried out using off-budget mechanisms. For illustration, Manzano et al. (2010) estimate the cost of the off-budget social and infrastructure expenditure programs of PDVSA at US$66.2 billion over 2003–08.

3. The papers by Davis, Ossowski, and Fedelino (2003) and Ossowski et al. (2008) provide a useful overview of the literature

and country experiences on special fiscal institutions to manage commodity (oil) revenues and are used extensively as background for this section. An examination of general fiscal rules by the IMF (2009c) also provides a comprehensive discussion on their evolution, design, implementation, and impact on fiscal performance.

4. For an overview and insights on the difficult choices official institutions face in managing their sovereign wealth, see Johnson-Calari and Rietveld (2007).

5. There is conflicting evidence on whether such strategies are effective at smoothing consumption (see, e.g., Rosenzweig and Binswanger 1993; Rosenzweig and Wolpin 1993; Fafchamps, Udry, and Czukas 1998; Dercon 2004).

6. Each of the inflation targeters (IT) in the region had positive correlations between dollar import prices and the dollar values of their currencies over the period 2000–08. In fact, these were greater than the correlations during the pre-IT period. The implication seems to be that the CPI they target does not, in practice, entirely exclude oil price shocks.

CHAPTER 6

Environmental and Social Consequences of Commodity Production

Key messages: Natural resource–based industries commonly impose costs on the environment and nearby populations. The reason for this varies depending on the nature of the activity and the policy environment in which it is carried out. Some resources—including fisheries and forests on public lands—are common property and therefore subject to overexploitation beyond a sustainable level of production. For others, such as minerals and hydrocarbons, production processes generate wastes, which are discarded into the environment, degrading it and imposing costs on populations who depend on environmental services for their livelihoods. This has led to significant social conflict over the years in a number of countries. For some commodity production—agriculture in particular—environmental problems are exacerbated by subsidies that encourage overuse of chemicals or overexploitation of scarce water resources.

Commodity production differs from other economic activities in two other important dimensions: First, it typically relies on public or common property resources (e.g., public forests, fishery stocks, hydrocarbon pools), where rights of exploitation and development are granted through concession or license agreements, which are in turn intended to generate public resources through royalties and tax arrangements. Second, in the presence of weak public institutions, inappropriate technologies, or ineffective regulatory enforcement, commodity production processes may generate significant negative environmental or social externalities, the true economic costs of which are not reflected in commodity prices. Under such conditions, rates of natural resource exploitation may both be unsustainable and generate large environmental and social costs—often multigenerational—for society, as has been the case in many LAC countries.

A comprehensive understanding of the risks and consequences of commodity production should encompass a review of all phases of production and extraction, processing, manufacturing, transport, waste disposal, and (where necessary) decommissioning. Although such a detailed analysis lies beyond the scope and means of this report, to illustrate the type and extent of the environmental and social challenges faced in commodity production, we focus on the exploitation of natural resources in four sectors: mining, oil, agriculture, and fisheries.

Mining

It is useful to compare and contrast two basic types of mine operations, which are associated with different environmental and social risks: large-scale industrial mining, such as for copper, silver, gold, lead, or zinc; and small-scale artisanal mining, in particular artisanal gold mining, which is commonplace in the Amazon Basin.

Large-scale mining

All large-scale mining methods involve some disturbance of the land surface and underlying strata, as well as some degree of degradation of surface and underground water resources. Exploration and predevelopment impacts are usually moderate and short term, and include a diverse array of potential impacts such as surface disturbance from access roads, drill holes and test pits, and site preparation; airborne dust from road traffic, drilling, excavating, and site clearing; noise and emissions from diesel equipment operation, blasting, and traffic; disturbance of soil and vegetation, streams, drainage, wetlands, groundwater aquifers, cultural resources, religious resources, and historic resources; and conflicts with other land uses.

Impacts become larger during the exploitation phase. Surface mining involves, among other activities, the drainage of the mine area and discharge of mine waters, the removal and storage or disposal of large volumes of solid waste material, and the removal and processing of the ore. The range of environmental concerns in surface mining includes immediate concerns about airborne particulates from road traffic, blasting, excavation, and materials transport; air emissions from various point sources; and noise and vibrations from heavy equipment and blasting. They also include concerns about longer-term damages stemming from discharges of contaminated mine water impacting downstream water users, failure of containment and discharge of tailings materials, use of scarce surface and groundwater aquifers for processing, disruption and contamination of groundwater aquifers, and removal of soil and vegetation.

In recent years, many large mining companies have come to realize that it is in their long-term interests to behave in environmentally (and socially) responsible ways. In Chile in the 1990s, for example, while the country was developing its legal and institutional frameworks, large mining companies voluntarily committed to substantive voluntary environmental agreements (IFC 2002). There is also some empirical evidence that this need not negatively impact companies' bottom lines. One study found that top environmental performers among the mining companies worldwide posted returns 60 percent higher over a three year period than those that were classified as poor performers (IFC 2002). There nonetheless remain numerous instances of negative consequences of mining that need to be addressed through governmental action.

Small-scale mining

Unlike large-scale producers, small-scale artisanal producers are often beyond the reach of policy and regulations. There are an estimated 400,000 artisanal gold miners in the Amazon Basin. They tend to be seasonal, highly mobile miners who have no security over their gold workings and are subject to displacement by larger "formal" mining operators. In small-scale mining, mercury escaping into the environment as a result of inadequate mining technology and poor practice during gold recovery generate the greatest environmental damage. It has been estimated that about 200 tons of mercury are still being released into the environment in the LAC region annually, and that as much as 10,500 tons of mercury may have been discharged or emitted to natural and urban environments from 1980 to 2007. Other environmental impacts of artisanal mining (and of alluvial mining in general) are soil degradation, deforestation, watercourse destabilization, stream-bed siltation, and significant loss of stream productivity.

The lack of ownership rights contributes to the environmental damage, because miners have a strong incentive to exploit their "holdings" as quickly as possible and cannot use land as collateral to finance investments in improving their production technology. In Peru, the fifth-largest gold producer in the world, it is estimated that about 40 percent of the production is informal or illegal, and few artisanal miners have tenure over their workings, which may be expropriated by larger commercial operations without compensation. The informal and illegal nature of artisanal mining also means that significant public revenue in the form of royalties and taxes has seldom been captured.

Oil Production

Environmental problems associated with hydrocarbon production are often a result of the disposal of by-products of the production process. Oil production can also foster the emergence of new social problems through vast migration toward oil-producing areas, not only of workers directly or indirectly involved with oil production, but also of many landless poor who take advantage of new land made accessible by the many roads opened by oil companies.

The high costs of remediating environmental damages caused by improper oil extraction also call for investing in environmentally sound extraction technologies. A case study of Ecuador highlights the main environmental challenges and cost implications:

- *Waste pits contaminated with oil or drilling mud.* In Ecuador, there are 346 confirmed and another 254 potential such sites in the Amazon. Through July 2006, 60 had been cleaned up at a cost of less than $90,000 each, implying a potential total cost of $54 million.

- *Unremediated spills.* Out of 542 spills recorded in the Amazónico district between January 2003 and August 2006, 44 percent were caused by corrosion, 28 percent by sabotage, 11 percent by equipment failure, and 8 percent by human error. Petroecuador has spent $54 million in the last three years to control spills and carry out cleanup and remediation of affected areas, including providing compensation to people affected by the spills. Systematic evidence is lacking as to the cleanup cost, but the remediation cost for two spills that have been studied are over $900,000 and $2.5 million. There is therefore a case for investing in technology to prevent such spills or limit the damage at an early stage; this would require pressure monitoring systems to detect ruptures and leaks. Extrapolating from one early project, it would cost about $60.8 million to implement automated monitoring, early alert, and rapid response systems in all of Petroecuador's fields in the Amazónico district. Currently, only the Trans-Ecuadorian Oil Pipeline System (SOTE) has such a system, although others are at various stages of implementation.

- *Discharge of untreated produced water.* Although there has been progress on reinjecting much of the wastewater generated back into the ground, there

is evidence that Petroecuador generates 29,000 gallons a day more than its reinjection capacity.

- *Installations decommissioned or abandoned without proper planning.* There has been no systematic inventory, but some of the sites on the Santa Elena Peninsula, for instance, will continue to pose a serious hazard for some time.

- *Flaring of associated gas.* Around 52 percent of gas associated with oil extraction is vented or burned, causing environmental problems and severe economic losses: the volume of gas lost each year at the oil fields in the Amazon is greater than that produced by the Amistad field for electricity generation.

Agriculture

Environmental impacts associated with agricultural commodities are diverse but typically include air and water pollution from production and processing as well as issues associated with unsustainable utilization of land resources and loss of natural habitats. Damages associated with conversion of land use (for example from forests to agriculture) or shifts from one sector to another (for example from livestock grazing to soy production) are often caused or greatly exacerbated by ill-considered public policies, which can reinforce the perverse incentives resulting from the common property nature of the resource or lead to unintended consequences through inappropriate subsidies. For example, although the causes of deforestation in the Amazon region are complex, nonexistent or insecure land tenure has been a contributing factor. And subsidies drive many of the most environmentally destructive practices. One example is the electricity subsidy to water extraction in Mexico (box 6.1).

Fisheries

Latin America and the Caribbean have some of the world's largest fisheries, as well as an increasingly important aquaculture industry. Peru's anchoveta fishery is the world's largest single species fishery, and Chile's aquaculture industry has also seen large foreign investments and market capture. But sustainable use of these key natural resources faces a range of challenges that demand sound policies, enhanced environmental

BOX 6.1

Environmentally Perverse Subsidies: Electricity Fees for Irrigators in Mexico

One of the biggest environmental challenges for Mexico is its unsustainable use of water, in particular groundwater. As of 2008, Mexico had 104 aquifers in unsustainable overexploitation, with extraction exceeding natural recharge, a problem compounded by growing populations and increasing economic activity. Moreover, the volume of water being extracted in these aquifers is estimated at nearly 200 percent of the average recharge, rapidly dropping water table levels and resulting in saline intrusion and the presence of heavy metals in some cases. This situation is of special concern because almost all cities in Mexico use groundwater as their main source of supply for households and industry, whereas nearly half of all irrigated agricultural production uses groundwater either as its single source or with water from dams.

Agriculture consumes more than 70 percent of the available freshwater in Mexico. The excess demand for water in this sector is caused by several factors, including the setting of electricity tariffs at highly subsidized levels, which increases the quantity of groundwater farmers wish to extract. Farmers with concessions pay only between US$0.02 and US$0.03 for each kilowatt-hour (kWh) they use, out of an average cost of generation and transmission of US$1.13 per kWh. In 2008, this implicit subsidy cost the government more than US$640 million.

A series of studies conducted by the Instituto Nacional de Ecología (INE), the policy research branch of the Mexican Ministry of the Environment, point to the electricity subsidy as causing not only significantly more extraction for a given distribution of farm technologies, but also greatly reducing the rate of adoption of water-saving irrigation technologies (INE 2005). This explains in part why, in Mexico, nearly 75 percent of farmers have dirt canals, the least efficient irrigation technology, even in regions with high water scarcity. These canals lose to evaporation and seepage one-third of the water pumped before it arrives to the crops. The INE estimates that, were the electricity subsidy to be completely eliminated, groundwater extraction would be reduced by 2,988 million liters per year, enough to bring back one of every four overexploited aquifers to a sustainable extraction path. Another feature of the electricity subsidy is that its distribution is highly unequal. Approximately 51 percent of all the funds go to the richest 10 percent of farmers (INE 2005). Such gross inequality would be at least politically controversial but for the fact that it is hidden in the apparently fair feature of having all farmers pay the same low fee.

Source: Carlos Muñoz of INE, Mexico, with World Bank staff.

governance, and regional cooperation. Ocean fisheries are classic cases of a common property resource and are prone to overexploitation. In the case of Peru's anchovetas, this is exacerbated by the El Niño cycle, which can change the yields from 2 million to 8 million tons. High variability has resulted in overfishing and in the past has caused a decline in the anchoveta stock, which took years to recover, plunging the industry into debt. Chile's salmon farming industry has also recently experienced major losses stemming partly from poor environmental monitoring, which led to rapid spread of salmon diseases. Similar governance weaknesses have previously caused economic and environmental losses in Ecuador's shrimp aquaculture. As is the case with agriculture, problems of overexploitation of deep-sea fisheries are exacerbated by the subsidies given by

many countries, especially high-income countries, to their fleets.

Social Impacts of Commodity Production

Commodity production activities, such as mining and oil production, have high potential to generate social tensions and conflicts. Often these are by-products of the adverse environmental impacts. Mining has a particularly negative reputation, stemming in part from its historical roots in the region. Large-scale mining in the Andes began after the looting of Inca treasures and involved one of the most exploitative treatments of indigenous people, the "mita," compulsory work in the gold and silver mines. Andean folklore, mythology, and poetry show that resentment still runs deep. In a number of cases, mining-related conflicts have turned violent (box 6.2).

BOX 6.2

Examples of Social Conflicts in Peru during the Last Decade

- Arequipa Region. The Peruvian government is promoting the formalization of a number of informal miners who produce around $800 million in annual revenues, saying that informal mining activities pollute rivers, destroy the environment, and create natural disasters due to lack of proper technology. The miners also support a legal formalization, but with rules that promote their small businesses. Instead of open dialogue to find common ground, this disagreement has resulted in conflict. In April 2010, miners blocked the Pan-American road in the Arequipa region. In a clash with police forces, 6 people were killed, 29 injured, dozens detained, and thousands more left stranded on the highway. The conflict remains unresolved; there is the possibility of an indefinite strike that may mobilize thousands of informal miners nationwide.

- Amazon Region. Since 2008, indigenous communities have protested against new laws that they believe would allow oil and mining companies to enter their territories without seeking consent or consultation. In June 2009, the protests culminated in a serious clash in Bagua where people were killed and injured. After this confrontation, the government canceled some of the decrees, but many remained in force. Local communities still demand that the government withdraw the remaining laws and reduce charges against indigenous leaders who are claimed to be responsible for the violent events. In general, the sentiment is that these projects have disrupted their lives and contaminated their environment, while their living standards have not improved.

- Huancabamba (Rio Blanco). This mine project is in a region that relies on raising cattle and growing crops for export. Since the beginning of the project, communities have worried about the potential destruction of the local ecosystem and the effect on the health of the people, livestock, and crops. In addition, they say the mining company did not comply with laws requiring the consent of the communities to start explorations in their territories. In 2005, during a peaceful demonstration, two people were killed and many others were injured. In 2007, the governments

of the affected communities held a referendum to let citizens express their opinion on the issue. The vast majority voted against the project, but the referendum was declared illegal. Hostility arose again when, in 2009, the police were accused of illegally holding protestors following the 2005 protest. In December 2009 two people were killed and several were wounded in a confrontation between local residents and the police.

- La Oroya. La Oroya is a smelter and refinery town, declared by the Blacksmith Institute to be one of the 10 most polluted places in the world. When Doe Run Peru (DRP) got the company, it agreed to an environmental management program (PAMA). In 2004 DRP indicated that it could not comply with its PAMA. The citizens, fearing that they could lose their jobs, demanded that the smelter be allowed to continue to operate. As a result, DRP was granted an extension. This highlights the tension between protecting the environment and protecting livelihoods.

- Cajamarca (Yanacocha). The Yanacocha gold mine has been involved in several social conflicts involving pollution of water supplies. In 2000, for example, a load of mercury was accidentally spilled, contaminating some towns in the region. According to government estimates, more than 900 people were poisoned. In 2004, the exploration of Cerro Quilish had to be suspended when local people protested that the project could damage their water supplies. Similarly in 2006, a conflict started over the construction of a dam in a nearby river. The inhabitants protested against possible contamination of water and the unfair distribution of social and economic benefits of the project. The protests ended in clashes between police and local farmers, after which one person was reported dead and many wounded. The government sent a commission to broker talks between the stakeholders; in the end, an agreement was reached.

Sources: Anaya (2001); Borum (2009); CATAPA (2009); Janssens (2009); London Mining Network (2009); Peruanista (2009); Salazar (2007); the View from Peru (2010); Vasquez (2010); World Bank (2005).

The common denominator of socially conflictive situations is the lack of trust among stakeholders, often justified by a history of poor environmental and social practices in natural resource exploitation, which has made dialogue difficult to achieve. Among the most common social issues are unfulfilled expectations for employment and benefits; land acquisition and resettlement impacts; lack of adequate communication in licensing processes; weak enforcement of regulations or absence of the government; lack of local capacity for negotiating and management; and the negative social perception of commodity production as a polluting activity that adversely affects public health.

Land acquisition, in particular, often ends up creating tensions, misunderstandings, and social conflicts. When land is purchased from peasants, even at reasonable compensation prices, they often do not know how to establish new livelihoods, and so they become landless rural workers who are usually ranked among the poorest of the poor. There are also several other factors that can further complicate land acquisition processes, such as unresolved conflicts over boundaries; lack of legal possession; difficulties in assessing market price; difficulties in assessing principles of reciprocity and land sharing among different communities; and the treatment of communal land versus individual land. To make things worse, the law may be used as a mechanism to exert pressure over those communities that do not agree on a contract for the purchase or use of their land. For instance, the Peruvian Law 26570 on *servidumbre minera* (Mining Easement Covenant 1996) is perceived with hostility among communities because it creates the perception that, if negotiations fail between the investor and the community, the latter will be the losers (World Bank 2005). A related difficulty for affected communities is the absence of support (if not outright hostility) of government at the local level.

Commodity-related activities alone cannot and should not, however, be expected to solve the complex issue of sustainability of the services and goods that they provide to local communities. Commodity production activities, such as mining and oil production, usually take place in remote and economically depressed areas, where government presence is sporadic, employment rates are low, and education is of poor quality. These factors explain the high expectations that local people have regarding commodity-related investments. In particular, these investments are seen as a source of job creation and as a means to obtain access to basic public services. Expectations have been fulfilled sometimes through community programs; however, commodity-related activities alone cannot solve local problems such as unemployment. Generally, after the investment phase, these types of activities require only specialized employees; however, most potential local workers lack the specific training and education to prepare them to become qualified workers. In order to solve the sustainability problems faced by local communities, government intervention and commitment are crucial.

CHAPTER 7

Conclusions and Policy Implications

Commodity Curse?

A key finding of this report is that the weight of econometric evidence and of case studies of the historical record indicate that the "commodity curse" (that natural resource abundance undercuts long-run growth), if it exists at all, is neither strong nor inevitable. The preponderance of the evidence indicates that resource wealth, on average, neither undermines nor disproportionately promotes economic growth. Nor, it seems, is there any "political curse" (that natural resource abundance weakens democratic institutions and fuels large-scale conflict), at least not in LAC. But even if there is no commodity curse, there are plenty of commodity concerns, which create significant risks. If not managed properly, these can adversely affect a country's prospects for economic and institutional development. Addressing them requires policy decisions on multiple fronts.

Putting the Dutch Disease in Perspective

Economic forces tend to reduce incentives for engaging in activities outside the resource sector: the "Dutch disease." This can be viewed as a natural manifestation of the principle of comparative advantage, and in that sense, it is not necessarily bad. Commodity production is not inherently inferior to other sectors in its potential for increased value added as production moves up the quality ladder, positive economic spillovers, social externalities, or development of linkages upstream and downstream. But weak diversification of exports—particularly in its extreme form—exacerbates the adverse economic effects of volatility, including negative effects on growth prospects. For this reason, it may be prudent to take measures to ameliorate somewhat the effects of Dutch disease and diversify the production structure of the economy.

Broadly speaking, there are two kinds of policy levers for this objective, which must operate in a complementary manner. One is the use of macroeconomic policy instruments, such as stabilization and sovereign wealth funds, to mitigate excessive exchange rate appreciations by managing fiscal volatility (discussed first below) and long-run assets. Trade liberalization can also counteract exchange rate appreciation. A second type of policy lever is non-exchange-rate-related measures to improve productivity and increase competitiveness.

Managing Fiscal Policy

From a strategic perspective, two major objectives of fiscal policy in commodity-dependent economies are to smooth out public expenditures in the short term in the face of volatile commodity-related revenues and to manage the wealth optimally in the long term. While policy instruments have often conflated these two objectives, they are conceptually distinct and could be managed with different tools. A third major objective is to reduce revenue volatility itself by diversifying the tax base and, when feasible, using insurance instruments. In line with general principles of behavior in response to risk (Becker and Ehrlich 1972), the optimal strategy is likely to involve a diversified approach, combining elements of all of these.

Managing short-term cycles

Insulating expenditures from boom-bust cycles of commodity revenues ideally calls for the use of a cyclically adjusted fiscal target combined with a stabilization fund that forces the accumulation of savings during commodity windfalls, which can then be used to stabilize spending in times of commodity busts. Thus, a stabilization fund can fulfill an expenditure stabilization function and contribute to a more effective countercyclical fiscal policy function.

The rules of stabilization funds governing accumulation and decumulation should take into account the objective of improving competitiveness, or at least of preventing excessive loss of exchange rate competitiveness for the noncommodity tradable sectors. This includes ex ante rules and decisions on *how much* to spend. The more of a windfall that is saved and invested offshore, the less pressure there will be on the real exchange rate to appreciate, simplifying monetary and fiscal policy. It also involves decisions on *how* to spend. Governments in developing countries will have many priority areas with high potential payoffs: for example, infrastructure projects, education, health, and social assistance. But large increases in domestic spending will overheat the economy and again appreciate the real exchange rate. Spending on projects with a high proportion of nontradable inputs will exacerbate this effect. For example, building more schools at home will appreciate the exchange rate more than will a program that finances scholarships for students to study abroad. Decisions on what to do with the proceeds of booms may also be shaped by the necessity of maintaining political support for the fund or fiscal rule.

Stabilization funds are generally commodity price or revenue contingent (e.g., in Mexico, Russia, Trinidad and Tobago, and República Bolivariana de Venezuela). The fund accumulates resources when the commodity price is higher than the reference value, and the fund contributes to budgetary resources when prices are lower. A critical challenge is choosing the reference commodity price. The reference value is most often preannounced in order to ensure transparency. It may be fixed in nominal terms or changed on a discretionary basis, and it is usually based on past observations combined with projected future prices. If contingent stabilization funds incorporate inflexible rules regarding the commodity reference price to use, the funds may be difficult to operate because long-run prices and quantities of extractable resources are hard to predict. The level of the fund relative to a desired level should also be taken into account in designing the accumulation-decumulation rules. This would force a faster accumulation (or slower decumulation) if the fund level were low, and would taper down the required accumulation (or allow greater decumulation) if the fund were near its desired level.

A certain degree of discretion over time regarding the choice of a reference price (or the desired level of the fund) is generally advisable. If the reference price is estimated inflexibly using historical data, then the actual commodity price conditions that emerge could render the fund unsustainable. In fact, the nature of the stochastic process that commodity prices seem to follow (a random walk) virtually ensures that any inflexible reference price would eventually cause the fund to either accumulate indefinitely or become exhausted. Box 7.1 lays out some lessons in good practice for incorporating these principles in designing such schemes.

Decisions to save a lot during a boom have proven to be politically challenging in LAC, resulting in numerous examples of stabilization funds or fiscal rules that have been abandoned in the face of pressure to spend. These pressures are amplified when political regimes lack credibility, and they consequently have short time horizons. Citizens sometimes will not trust their governments to deliver on promises of future spending in the citizens' interests and may even fear that the money in a stabilization fund will vanish. This underscores the importance of governance—particularly in ensuring transparency and accountability in revenue management—a subject discussed below.

When governments do enjoy a degree of credibility, the stabilization measures may receive more broad-based support if voters know the proceeds will be linked to something important in their lives—for example, increased social spending during the inevitable bust part

BOX 7.1

Key Design Elements for a Natural Resource Fund

- **Ensure the fund is well integrated within the budget.** The fund should operate as a government account rather than a separate institution. The operation of two different resource and nonresource budgets should be avoided because it could compromise transparency and lead to fiscal management problems. A unified fiscal framework should therefore be the aim. The better integrated a fund is within the budget, the better coordinated will be fiscal use of resource and nonresource revenues.

- **Include the fund in the asset and liability management framework of the government.** The asset management strategy for the fund should be well aligned with the corresponding public-sector debt strategy.

- **Align the investment strategy of the fund with its aims.** The investment strategy should target the desired levels of risk and liquidity. The risk profiles of investments are important; for a natural resource fund focused on stabilization, its reserves

should be available for withdrawal on short notice, and even relatively low-risk, long-term equities may not fit with the fund's objective. By contrast, an intergenerational savings fund can have a longer-term investment strategy.

- **Ensure that the fund has no authority to spend.** To prevent fragmentation of policy making and loss of overall fiscal control, it is preferable that a fund not have a mandate to spend—and if it does, then any extra- or off-budget spending should be subject to parliamentary consideration.

- **Ensure transparency of fund activities.** Rules should ensure transparency, good governance, and accountability to prevent misuse of resources. There should be frequent disclosure of fund activities, inflows and outflows, the allocation of assets, and the profiles of investments.

Sources: Davis, Ossowski, and Fedelino (2003); Ossowski et al. (2008); Das et al. (2009) (this piece provides a good discussion of design and operation issues).

of the cycle, or reinforcement of the pension system. Chile's experience over the recent price cycle illustrates the political benefits of saving during good times in order to fund social programs during the inevitable downside of the cycle (see box 7.2). After the crash, the presidential approval rate skyrocketed in Chile, while plummeting in other commodity-producing countries (figure 7.1).

There will inevitably be trade-offs among competing spending goals, and between the welfare of current and future generations. And the socially optimum solution will depend, to some extent, on the structure of the economy. Certainly there is no one-size-fits-all prescription, but the process of deciding on the trade-offs should be insulated as much as possible from short-term political pressures. The use of independent advisory boards of experts, as exemplified by fiscal councils, may be useful in this regard.

Fiscal councils or independent fiscal agencies can increase the political cost of inappropriate management

of natural resource revenues. As described by Debrun, Hauner, and Kumar (2007), fiscal councils are nonpartisan bodies that provide independent input into the budgetary processes. In commodity-reliant economies, one critical area where fiscal councils can contribute is in providing unbiased estimates of commodity prices for use in budget planning. This would get around the problem of manipulating the commodity reference price used to formulate the budget to suit political objectives. A case in point is Chile, where two independent panels of experts come up with estimates for trend GDP and the long-term reference price of copper, for use as inputs for calculating the structural balance target for the budget.

Sustaining real wealth over the long term

Countries' prospects for long-run sustainable growth are diminished by resource extraction to the extent that the value of the resources extracted is not compensated by accumulating alternative assets, such as

BOX 7.2

Fiscal Rules as Social Policy

Engel, Nielsen, and Valdés (2010) examine the role of fiscal policy across the cycle when there are exogenously driven (e.g., commodity-driven) and volatile fiscal revenues. They present a theoretical model in which there is a substantial welfare gain associated with running a countercyclical fiscal policy that targets increased spending to the poor. Their model is motivated by fiscal savings in Chile during the recent copper revenue boom that enabled the government to put in place a substantial and well-targeted fiscal package beginning in 2008. As part of the fiscal stimulus, the Chilean government made one-off transfers to the poorest 40 percent in March and August 2009. For the poorest decile, these transfers equaled about two months of income.

In the model, households have incomes that fluctuate across the commodity cycle. The government planner in the model is focused on managing fiscal transfers so as to maximize household utility over time. Because of revenue uncertainty, precautionary savings are made in good times to finance transfers to households in bad times. Inequality in household income is critical in the model. Equal incomes means that there is a representative agent that receives average income, whereas inequality (heterogeneity) introduces a poorer population with less stable marginal utility over time.

Incorporating heterogeneity in household income introduces an important role for targeting in the context of fiscal policy. With no targeting, an optimal policy rule would be more expensive in bad times because spending would need to be higher to achieve the same level of welfare compared to a situation where transfers can be targeted to the needy. Conversely, the greater the possibility to target the poor in bad times, the lower the amount of government spending required. The larger and more volatile the commodity revenues, the higher are the welfare gains associated with adopting an optimal "social needs" rule over a balanced budget expenditure. Welfare gains are greater the better is targeting in bad times, but they are smaller when there is no heterogeneity between household income levels.

A calibration of the model for Chile suggests that the government should spend 100 percent of revenues in very low revenue states, but less that 100 percent even in slightly below-the-mean states (due to the precautionary saving motives). Around 80 percent should be saved in the most favorable states.

Source: Engel, Nielsen, and Valdés (2010).

FIGURE 7.1

Economic Management Rewarded? Presidential Approval Ratings in Bolivia, Chile, Ecuador, and República Bolivariana de Venezuela

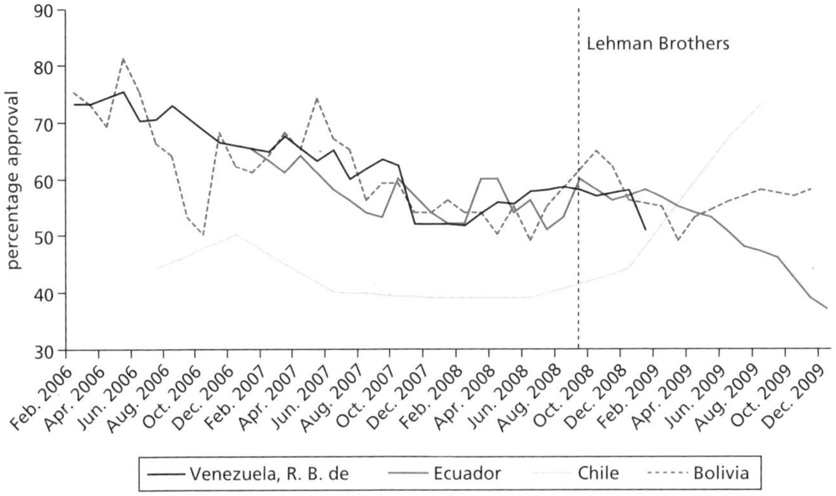

Sources: Chile: Engel, Nielsen, and Valdés (2010); for Bolivia: Mori, Gallup, and Apoyo agencies (available months included); for República Bolivariana de Venezuela and Ecuador: CEDATOS, *Estudios & Datos*, Quito, Enero 2010.

human, financial, or physical forms of capital, or by paying down burdensome liabilities. A key policy message for commodity-dependent countries with a high value of resource extraction is that public expenditure and other policies need to encourage a high rate of saving and investment to avoid running down the stock of real wealth over time. One rule for achieving "optimal" intertemporal use (under certain assumptions) is to invest all of the proceeds of exhaustible resource extraction in human or physical capital. This is the Hartwick rule, discussed in chapter 3.

Of course, optimal decisions on how to distribute wealth over time are complex and depend on country-specific circumstances. For poor countries, the discount rate or return on spending money now rather than later may be very high, and it may be hard to justify saving the bulk of the resources for future generations if they can be effectively used to raise current living standards. When a country has high public-sector debt levels or contingent liabilities, moreover, there may be a higher social return associated with paying off burdensome debts or making provisions, for example, for future pension liabilities. But for other countries, especially those affected by high inequality and social exclusion syndromes, the social debt may take priority, increasing the premium on using the natural resource rents to explicitly address problems of social injustice and close the gap between the "have-nots" and the "haves." Recent political developments in Bolivia, Ecuador, and República Bolivariana de Venezuela reflect, in part, the struggle to use natural resource rents to address social needs, even at the risk of creating macroeconomic imbalances or weakening the investment climate.

Still, even taking all of the complexities into account, it will generally be in a country's long-term interests to save a substantial part of commodity rents. Many countries have used a sovereign wealth fund as a way to maintain high savings. This has often been combined with a stabilization fund, but it need not be. And because the asset composition and management strategies for long-run wealth accumulation are likely to differ from those for short-term goals, there may be advantages in splitting the two.[1] Policies that encourage private savings will also help preserve a country's real stock of wealth.

However, it has often been the case, at least partially because of unproductive choices in public spending, that countries with high resource rents tend to end up with lower "genuine savings rates"—that is, they consume more than the value of the resources they are extracting, thereby depleting their total stock of capital. Unfortunately, the relationship in LAC countries (figure 7.2) seems very similar to that in other countries.

In making public expenditure choices to maintain real wealth, a particular concern in LAC is the heavy use of subsidies to lower energy prices. As noted, energy price subsidies are large (more than 2 percent of GDP on average in LAC), regressive, nontransparent, and unproductive. For several countries, they are higher than expenditures on education. Eliminating or improving the targeting of energy price subsidies could free up fiscal resources to make productive investments in physical and human capital to replace the real wealth lost in nonrenewable resource extraction.

Reforming these subsidy policies has proven politically difficult, and innovative approaches are needed to overcome the impasse. Mexico is exploring a new approach to phasing out energy subsidies based on the principle of decoupled payments, as used in the

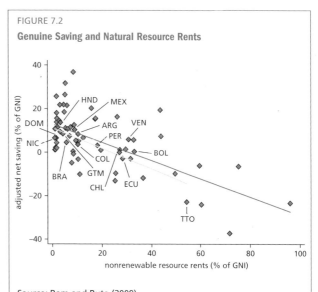

FIGURE 7.2

Genuine Saving and Natural Resource Rents

Source: Ram and Ruta (2009).
Notes: ARG = Argentina; BRA = Brazil; BOL = Bolivia; CHL = Chile; COL = Colombia; DOM = Dominican Republic; ECU = Ecuador; GTM = Guatemala; HND = Honduras; MEX = Mexico; NIC = Nicaragua; PER = Peru; TTO = Trinidad and Tobago; VEN = República Bolivariana de Venezuela.

reform of agricultural subsidies in many countries, which may have wider applicability (box 7.6). As with the stabilization funds and fiscal rules, improving public expenditures requires government credibility. Citizens who do not trust the government's promises may understandably prefer that rents be dissipated immediately, even as inefficient subsidies, rather than taking their chances that the money will be managed well in the future.

Reducing revenue volatility

In addition to insulating expenditures from the volatility of revenue streams, governments can reduce the volatility of the revenues directly. Market-supplied

---

BOX 7.3

IBRD Commodity Products and Services

Commodity Swaps: IBRD currently offers borrowers access to financial products to manage risks related to commodity price volatility. This product gives borrowers the opportunity to protect themselves from exposure to commodity price risk by effectively linking the repayment obligations of IBRD loans to a commodity price or index. For a country or borrower that is exposed to the risk of commodity price increases (i.e., a consumer), the loan could be structured so that repayment of the principal or the interest rate would decrease if commodity prices increase. For a country or borrower that is exposed to the risk of commodity price declines (i.e., a producer), the loan could be structured so that repayment of the principal or the interest rate would decrease if commodity prices decrease.

An IBRD loan structured this way would have two components:

- An existing IBRD loan, with corresponding LIBOR-based interest rate, maturity, and repayment characteristics.
- An overlying commodity swap transaction that exchanges the cash flows of the original IBRD loan for a new set of cash flows based on an interest rate and repayment profile that incorporates the costs and potential payouts of a commodity swap. The commodity swap would establish the desired price protection.

Borrowers evaluating this instrument would need to consider (1) how much of the exposure to commodity price volatility to cover, (2) what price levels should be protected, and (3) the tenor or timeframe of the coverage. As a general rule, costs are higher for price protection for longer periods of time (i.e., 10 years forward) than they are for shorter timeframes (i.e., 1 to 5 years forward).

Advisory Services: An important first step in implementation of a commodity risk management strategy is a risk assessment process that quantifies how commodity price volatility directly or indirectly affects the government budget. From a fiscal perspective, commodity price movements can affect tax or royalty income, contingent liabilities associated with subsidy programs, stabilization funds, safety nets or support mechanisms, and in some cases support for emergency responses, for example in the case of food or energy insecurity. Because these issues can be complex, the World Bank Treasury offers advisory services on commodity risk management. Advisory engagements cover the following services:

- Risk assessment to identify and quantify direct or indirect impacts of price volatility on the budget
- Analysis of the existing institutional framework
- Technical support to design a framework for selecting hedging strategies
- Training of stakeholders and policy makers
- Technical support to build a robust infrastructure for hedging risk within a sound legal framework; appropriate credit risk management; adequate systems for booking, accounting, and valuation; and the oversight capabilities required for proper risk monitoring and management
- Structuring and execution of transactions with the market

The World Bank Treasury can provide assistance to member countries interested in commodity hedging and will work with countries to develop a customized strategy that meets specific needs.

Source: World Bank Treasury.

hedging instruments may help stabilize fiscal revenues. To be sure, the market for hedging the prices of oil and certain other minerals is relatively well developed, although the maturities tend to be shorter than a country would need. Governments have hedged commodity price risk on international futures markets with mixed results. There have been examples in which the use of derivatives was widely perceived as "successful." For example, Mexico's use of put options to hedge oil revenues in 2009 ended up creating a profit of around $5 billion, 0.9 percent of GDP.

But public misunderstandings and misperceptions about hedging have often led to political problems. Hedging is wrongly regarded as an opportunity for financial gain rather than as a form of insurance, so government officials may be blamed if it doesn't pay off. In contrast, if no insurance is sought and commodity prices later fall, it is easy to assign the blame to exogenous market conditions. This danger could be minimized with better education of the public and with legal protection for government officials acting in good faith. Following the US$5 billion profit from hedging in 2009, Mexico again hedged its 2010 production at an upfront cost of around US$1 billion. Agustin Carstens, head of the Central Bank and former minister of finance, went on record publicly explaining, "We want this as an insurance policy. If we don't collect any resources from this transaction, it's OK with us."[2] The usefulness of such instruments is, however, also limited by their relatively short-term nature. Decisions regarding whether and how best to use these instruments are complex, and the World Bank offers advisory services for governments interested in exploring these options, as well as one specific risk management instrument based on the use of "swaps," the commodity linked loan (box 7.3).

Improving Productivity in Commodity-Dependent Economies

The premium on undertaking dedicated actions to foster productivity growth is arguably greater in commodity-rich countries in order to offset the risk that a temporary commodity bonanza (and its associated Dutch disease effects) could permanently destroy tradable (exporting and import-competing) activities that

would otherwise be viable. Of course, the class of policies that directly or indirectly improve productivity and competitiveness is very large; arguably, almost all economic development policy falls under this rubric. De Ferranti et al. (2002) offer an extensive discussion of such policies, including measures to deepen opening to trade and foreign direct investment and to promote investments in human capital, knowledge generation, institutions, and public infrastructure.

But there are some policies and investments in public goods that focus squarely on this objective. For example, Chile's Innovation for Competitiveness Fund was established with a levy on mining revenues, and it may serve as a model for other commodity-dependent countries (box 7.4). In addition, it is worth underscoring that foreign direct investment often brings more than project funding. By introducing new technology and modern business management practices, it can also boost productivity. And it can be useful in scaling the quality ladder, as illustrated, for instance, by the development of the Chilean fruit and vegetable and salmon sectors.

In designing public expenditures and policies to encourage export diversification and technological innovation, the focus should be on promoting product-neutral incentives to support these objectives rather than on picking and then protecting specific "winner" products (Lederman and Maloney 2006). Basic research and knowledge generation are public goods that improve competiveness and productivity and have consistently been shown to have high rates of return. Realistically, of course, almost any public expenditure or regulatory innovation will benefit some sectors more than others, and so inevitably some "winners" will be picked. But the key is not to grant large subsidies and high protection, as has sometimes been done, but rather to create a healthy business environment that facilitates the discovery of profitable investment opportunities and ensures that markets remain open and contestable. Although spending on education is not aimed specifically at improving competitiveness, the findings of Brambilla and Porto (2009) are also relevant in the context of public expenditure policies in commodity-dependent economies. These authors found that skill premia are

BOX 7.4

Technological Innovation as a Means to Cope with Dutch Disease: The Chilean Experience

Chile's National Innovation System is a central part of a growth strategy launched by the government to generate a productive transformation of the Chilean economy. This box summarizes the main actions undertaken by Chile to enhance innovation, based on information from the World Bank (2010).

Since the creation of a Competitiveness and Innovation Fund in 2005, the Chilean government has dramatically increased its investment in the innovation sector at an annual rate of 24 percent, going from US$240 million in 2005 to US$530 million in 2009 (in 2009 US$).[3] This increase in budget has been financed through a royalty levy on the mining industry. The goal of the fund is to promote six strategic interests: entrepreneurial innovation, human capital formation, science and technology promotion, internationalization of innovative efforts, public awareness of innovation, and innovation in the public interest. In addition to increasing the resources devoted to innovation, the government has also carried out a series of institutional initiatives such as the creation of the National Innovation Council for Competitiveness, which is responsible for developing a national innovation strategy, and the creation of a Ministerial Committee for Innovation to ensure the implementation of the national innovation strategy at the ministerial level.

The national innovation strategy consists of four main institutional innovations. The first innovation focuses on identifying clusters with specific strategic areas of research. The second innovation focuses on increasing the participation of the private sector through technology consortia.

These groups have been set up as private entities with private companies, sector organizations, public technology institutes, or universities as shareholders. The groups are given start-up subsidies, but once initial subsidies expire, the members of the consortia are expected to finance the full costs. As of 2009, these consortia have contributed an estimated 15–20 percent of total public agricultural R&D investment. The third initiative is designed to build capacity to strengthen the competitiveness of clusters in cross-cutting areas such as biotechnology, environment and water resources, renewable energy, and information technology and communication. The support consists of core funding for research centers of excellence, which are managed as private enterprises during a given period of time; after this period, the centers have to obtain their own funding. To date, there are around 50 centers of excellence operating, and the majority of them are university based. The fourth initiative focuses on the allocation of funds through a competitive process.

To complement the innovation strategy, the government has also demonstrated a commitment to investment in human capital, with the launch of a Bicentenary Scholarship Fund (Fondo Bicentenario de Capital Humano) of US$6 billion to finance the development of professionals at the level of master's and doctorate degrees in overseas universities.[4] The key goal, among others, for 2010 is to have 3,300 professionals studying abroad, which would be a 672 percent increase over 2006.

Source: Authors, from World Bank (2010).

not systematically lower in commodity sectors, and therefore that returns to investments in education are high, regardless of the degree of commodity specialization of the economy.

Countries have often pursued diversification using policies that were not cost effective. One such misguided policy has been to grant some noncommodity sectors unduly high rates of effective protection. Although this might seem to avoid the worst symptoms of Dutch disease, the resulting diversification of tradable but sheltered activities is not likely to be sustainable if it cannot survive, sooner or later, in an open

economy. Experience with these policies has demonstrated that protected sectors have not contributed the most to economic diversification. Similarly, the provision of highly subsidized gas to the local petrochemical or other industries as a means to encourage diversification has, in some cases, led to growth, but at a high cost in lost export earning opportunities and discouragement of foreign investment—investors are reluctant to make commitments knowing that they will have to provide subsidized gas to domestic users.

In reality, what Justin Lin, the World Bank's chief economist, calls "comparative advantage–defying policies"—such as high protection or excessive subsidization of domestic activities—are unnecessary and are possibly counterproductive, particularly because, as shown, commodity sectors can organically develop forward and backward linkages with other sectors in the right institutional and business environment settings. This lesson is especially poignant in Latin America, where many countries in earlier decades tried to force industrialization in a wide range of sectors with little regard for real comparative advantage. As a result, several small countries had production structures similar to that of advanced industrial economies (Blomstrom and Meller 1991). Chile and Ecuador had as many car producers in the 1960s as the United States (De Ferrati et al. 2002)! This contributed to spectacular economic debacles in the later 1970s and 1980s. Blomstrom and Meller (1991) and De Ferranti et al. (2002) contrast this with the experience of many of today's high-income countries (Australia, Canada, Scandinavian countries, and the United States), where natural resource wealth provided the original basis of growth for the economies, which then diversified into resource-based manufacturing and eventually into other, more knowledge-intensive industries. One characteristic of economies that encouraged this evolutionary diversification was a high level of human capital, complemented by dense networks of institutions to generate and diffuse knowledge.

Although policies may foster the development of viable noncommodity sectors, they should not neglect the commodity sectors themselves. As noted, natural resource–based production can have linkages and positive externalities and can serve as a source of revenue, providing fiscal space for the government to foster efficient human and physical capital formation. Maloney (2007) argues that one reason Latin America has missed out on resource-based growth opportunities relates to deficiencies in technological adoption and adaptation. This has been the result of two factors: shortfalls in national learning or innovative capacity, arising from low investments in human capital, and the long period of inward-looking industrialization, which undermined the natural resource–intensive sectors and effectively killed (or at least injured) the

goose that laid the golden eggs (Lederman and Maloney 2009).

Even growth in commodity sectors can foster diversification. This message emerges from the distinction among the different channels through which concentration can create a bias against growth. The source of the bias is neither a lack of positive externalities nor declining terms of trade, but rather volatility of foreign exchange flows and fiscal revenues. This volatility can be reduced by diversification of the export basket into any products with which the current basket is not perfectly correlated or that have lower volatility than the current basket. This could include primary commodities that are not currently in the basket or downstream-processed products using the main commodity in the current basket, which generally have less volatile prices than the primary commodity itself.

Improving Governance in Commodity-Dependent Economies

As we have seen, many of the difficulties in optimal economic management of commodity wealth can be traced directly to credibility problems of governments. If citizens do not trust government promises to use well the resources that are saved for the future, they will not reward decisions that delay immediate gratification. The results are likely to be overexploitation of the resource and failure to save, both in the long term to preserve the real wealth of the country, and in the short term to break the boom-bust cycle. Enhancing credibility goes beyond policies affecting the natural resource sector, but some measures associated with resource governance could help.

Increasing transparency and accountability in managing natural resource rents (earnings and use)

Lack of transparency undermines the government's credibility with its citizens and magnifies the corrosive effects that commodity-related rents can have on institutions. In the case of LAC, many countries do not make publicly available data on the total natural resource rents (particularly hydrocarbon and mining rents) received by the national and subnational governments.

The Extractive Industries Transparency Initiative (EITI), which calls for the regular publication of an audited account of all oil, gas, and mining payments by companies to governments, is a potentially useful lever for increasing resource revenue transparency. Putting this information in the public domain allows for debate by all stakeholders (the government, opposition parties, and civil society) on the amount and use of revenues. So far, Peru is the only EITI candidate country in LAC (see box 7.5).[5]

Transparency in revenue collection must be accompanied by transparency in revenue distribution and management regimes. As noted by Dunning (2008), "revenue collection transparency must be matched by transparency in other parts of the [natural resource] value chain, particularly transparency for revenue distribution and management." For LAC,

this applies particularly to resources spent on energy subsidies, which consume a large chunk of budget resources for many of the region's commodity producers. These are generally implicit and therefore nontransparent. A reporting of the aggregate cost and incidence of these subsidies in the budget would make explicit the trade-off in lost opportunities (e.g., for increasing spending on education or health).

The analysis in this report also suggests that, to make the most of resource rents, a country may need to go beyond natural resource management tools to tackle the underlying institutions that shape how rents are used. Dunning (2008) notes that a lack of checks and balances on government impact negatively on natural resource rent outcomes. One way to improve this would be through a separation of power

---

BOX 7.5

Extractive Industries Transparency Initiative

The Extractive Industries Transparency Initiative (EITI) is a global standard for transparency for revenues from oil, gas, and mining. It sets a standard for companies to publish what they pay and for governments to disclose what they receive. The initiative was launched in 2002 and is overseen by the EITI board made up of 20 members from countries (implementing and supporting), companies, and civil society. It has a robust yet flexible methodology for monitoring and reconciling company payments and government revenues at the country level. The process in each country is overseen by participants from the government, companies, and national civil society. The EITI Board and the International Secretariat are the guardians of the EITI methodology internationally.

Implementation of EITI involves complying (according to an external verification process) with the following criteria:

- Regular publication of all material oil, gas, and mining payments by companies to governments ("payments") and all material revenues received by governments from oil, gas, and mining companies ("revenues") to a wide audience in a publicly accessible, comprehensive, and comprehensible manner.

- Where such audits do not already exist, payments and revenues are the subject of a credible, independent audit, applying international auditing standards.
- Payments and revenues are reconciled by a credible, independent administrator, applying international auditing standards and with publication of the administrator's opinion regarding that reconciliation including any identified discrepancies.
- This approach is extended to all companies including state-owned enterprises.
- Civil society is actively engaged as a participant in the design, monitoring, and evaluation of this process and contributes to public debate.
- A public, financially sustainable work plan for all the above is developed by the host government, with assistance from the international financial institutions where required; the plan includes measurable targets, a timetable for implementation, and an assessment of potential capacity constraints.

Source: http://eitransparency.org/eiti/principles.

between decision making on the size of rents and their allocation. For example, having an independent expert panel, as in Chile, which decides on the "above trend" natural resource windfall revenues, can be a useful device for increasing the accountability of government decision making. Such clear rules that improve transparency and accountability could do much to bolster credibility and allow the government to make believable promises, weakening the incentives that can lead to squandering of rents.

Breaking the cycle of ownership reversals of the natural resource sector (public to private and vice versa)

An inefficient cyclical pattern of nationalization and privatization has characterized the history of LAC's extractive industries and is one manifestation of the credibility problem. Nationalization tends to occur when the price of the corresponding commodity is high, and privatization tends to occur when it is low. But nationalization comes at a high cost, including a weakening of the credibility—and bargaining position—of the government relative to foreign investors in future negotiations. Because of past nationalization episodes, many countries were in a weak position in the 1990s and were forced to make greater concessions than they otherwise would have. They entered into unduly inflexible contractual arrangements with terms that, under subsequent high prices, seemed to their citizens to be overgenerous to the private sector. A lesson from this experience is that flexibility is key. Tax arrangements could reduce pressure to nationalize to the extent that they are flexible to changing commodity prices, thereby allowing governments to share in the upside. Contractual arrangements—perhaps through contingent clauses that allow the government to participate in the benefits from booming prices— could also be used for this purpose.

High levels of inequality or social marginalization and resentment of environmental impacts of the resource extraction are also associated with increased pressures for nationalization. An agenda that promotes equality of opportunity and improved social and environmental protection would help alleviate this. To this topic we now turn.

Achieving Environmentally and Socially Sound Resource Exploitation

Potential environmental impacts can be mitigated, and in some cases avoided, by good project planning and design. Beyond the design stage, measures to minimize environmental impacts can be grouped into four major categories: tools based on state regulation and oversight, reversal of counterproductive government policies, incentives and market-based enforcement, and enforcement by civil society and external stakeholders. Fisheries management is an interesting case that may combine elements of several of these.

Interventions based on state regulation and oversight

Under command-and-control approaches, governments can rely on several policy and legal tools. Some (criteria, objectives, guidelines, processes, and plans) may not be directly enforceable, but they nevertheless often provide the context for compliance and legal enforcement.

Instruments such as project permits, licenses, bans, and contracts will usually be enforceable, providing that they are issued under enabling legislation or that the government agency is legally mandated to issue contracts. Environmental permits created under legislation offer the opportunity to apply the "polluter-pays" principle, which bases the permit or license fee on environmental risks or on the quality of environmental performance. Designing and enforcing environmental standards in federalized systems may require building capacity at the local level. Argentina, with assistance from the World Bank in 1997, streamlined its mix of federal and provincial laws on mining and engaged in an intensive capacity-building program to assist each province in monitoring its own area (IFC 2002).

Local community fisheries management focuses on regulations specifying fishing gear, location, and timing. Explosives are seldom allowed, and the characteristics of fishing nets are regulated. There are permanent bans on catching certain species, such as turtles, and seasonal bans to allow stocks to grow. In general, regulations on allowable species and timing change according to ecological conditions and social needs.

Reforming counterproductive government policies

In some cases, environmental damage is the direct result of government incentives. The obvious solution is to remove the subsidy. This is the case, for example, when pesticides or other agricultural chemicals are subsidized. Use of these chemicals often produces negative external effects—pollution of surface water or aquifers, for example—and so there is a danger that they would be used more than is socially optimal in any case. But subsidization exacerbates this problem. The electricity subsidy to farmers to pump irrigation water from aquifers in some of the driest regions in Mexico is another example of a subsidy that encourages environmentally destructive practices. As with other subsidies, it has proven politically difficult to remove, but an innovative pilot program may provide a way forward and could be used as a model for reforming other subsidies (box 7.6).

Incentives and market-based enforcement

An alternative to the command-and-control approach is the use of market-based instruments to internalize negative (or positive) externalities by imposing appropriate taxes on the polluter (or by providing appropriate payments to those who provide environmental benefits). If the incentives are quantified and set correctly (which can be challenging), they will encourage all parties to behave in a way that results in the "correct" level of production and environmental impact. Incentives and market-based enforcement mechanisms include the following:

- *Charges.* Charges include transport charges for peak hour use of congested roads, harvesting taxes, stumpage fees for logging, water charges to regulate water quality, and waste charges. Often, revenues from charges are used to improve environmental standards or to remedy past environmental damages. Charges can also provide incentives to polluting producers to improve the environmental efficiency of production technologies.

- *Payments.* Payments work in the same way and have the same purpose as charges—that is, to provide incentives to use more environmentally friendly procedures and technologies—but they

---

BOX 7.6

Reforming Environmentally Perverse Subsidies through Decoupling: Electricity Fees for Irrigators in Mexico

As described above (box 6.1), the electricity subsidy to pump water for irrigation in some dry areas in Mexico is environmentally destructive and expensive. The need for reforming this policy has been evident for many years, but politically this has been difficult. The Mexican government is now trying a pilot program that would, if successful, offer a politically attractive solution. Farmers participating in the program would have to pay an unsubsidized price for electricity, but they would receive compensation through lump-sum payments, based, for example, on land area or historical usage. (This type of subsidy is called by the World Trade Organization and the OECD a "decoupled" subsidy.) Paying full price would remove the incentive to overexploit the aquifer, and the decoupled payment would make it easier to invest in water-saving technologies, especially for credit-constrained farmers. The strategy is to launch a small voluntary pilot project in 2010 in seven different aquifers to check the political acceptance of such a deal. It will be done following a quasi-experimental design, with a group of aquifers being offered the decoupling, another having an increased enforcement effort against illegal water extraction, a third group having both types of intervention, and a fourth acting as a control group. The pilot program will require farmers to invest their entire decoupled subsidy in new water-saving infrastructure or equipment. If successful, the pilot program could serve as the basis for designing a broader program, probably one that includes all overexploited aquifers.

Programs similar to this, based on decoupled payments, have been the key to reforming agricultural subsidies in many countries, both high-income and developing. This model could be useful in reforms of other forms of energy subsidies, which are so pervasive in LAC.

Source: Carlos Muñoz, with World Bank staff.

work by compensating producers rather than charging them. A special case of payments is the use of payments for environmental services (see box 7.7). Payments have several advantages over traditional approaches. First, they allocate money that was not previously available to conservation efforts. Second, they are efficient. In regulatory command-and-control approaches, the appropriate degree of reduction is difficult to establish. Even with a pollution tax, the economically efficient level is difficult for the regulator to know. When the payment mechanism is negotiated voluntarily between the provider and

user of environmental services, the two parties negotiate a price that reflects the true value of the service. This price should generally be renegotiated periodically, preferably yearly, in order to ensure that it is not out of line with the value of the service under changing circumstances.

- *Tradable permits.* Issuing permits to pollute at a predetermined level, while allowing trade in these permits, ensures that a given level of pollution reduction is achieved by the parties that can do it at lowest cost. This idea can also be applied to the use of natural resources. For instance, tradable quotas are used in fisheries management,

---

BOX 7.7

Payment for Environmental Services

Payment for environmental services (PES) is a mechanism used to improve the provision of indirect environmental services (Pagiola 2006). The main characteristics of a PES mechanism are that participation is generally voluntary, with payments negotiated between the providers and users of the services, and payments are made conditional upon an action taken or not taken (i.e., avoided deforestation or reforestation). Existing PES mechanisms finance the provision of four types of environmental services: improving water quality, reducing carbon emissions, preserving biodiversity, and preserving scenic beauty. Latin America has been a leader in developing these schemes. To date, there have been 122 mechanisms across Latin America and the Caribbean at some stage of implementation or planning or already completed. One important shortcoming of existing mechanisms is that monitoring is often not conducted, and consequently, little concrete information is available on actual results. The limited evidence suggests that water PES mechanisms have had some degree of success in mitigating sedimentation and distribution of agricultural chemicals, but even here, there is a great need for impact evaluation in order to be able to determine effectiveness.

So far, there have been relatively few cases in which PES-like mechanisms have been used to mitigate the environmental externalities of extractive industries. One example in Peru, however, suggests that there may be

some potential. The Jequetepeque project in Peru was developed by local communities in coordination with the World Wildlife Fund (WWF) and CARE to reforest an area that was contaminated by urban and mine effluents (WWF 2010). What is somewhat unique about this case is that the users are poor communities that do not have the funds to pay on their own for environmental services, and thus depend on external funding sources.

PES could also be a particularly attractive mechanism if there were other utilities or users located downstream from the mine, which would be willing to finance actions to reduce siltation, or if the mine were willing to pay upstream or downstream farmers to take action to offset discharge from the mine. How such a scheme might work is suggested by a study in southwest Zimbabwe, exploring the potential of payment for ecosystem services in connection with small-scale gold mining. Gold panning is a large revenue source for the community of Zhulube, but it can have negative effects on forest resources, boreholes, and river water quality and quantity (Nyamukure 2008). In order to address sedimentation control and water quality maintenance, the Nyamukure study looked at the possibility of providing incentives to upstream conservation farmers and gold panners from the community of Zhulube to protect water quality.

Sources: Nyamukure (2008); Organization of American States (2010); Pagiola (2006); World Wildlife Fund (2010).

and development rights are used to control urban sprawl and the growth of tourism infrastructure in fragile ecosystems. Other examples of transferable rights in natural resource management include water rights and grazing rights. The use of tradable quotas has significantly reduced overexploitation of fisheries, thereby increasing profits and stocks (most notably in Icelandic and New Zealand fisheries). However, the concentration of quotas in a few hands has produced social tension in some communities.

- *Institutional design.* Changes in institutional design can also improve producers' incentives to respect environmental standards. Options are specific to the local context, but there are many examples. They include the formalization of land or resource tenure to allow properties to be sold (mining claims) or used as collateral for financing; mobilization (financing and technical support) of grassroots nongovernmental organizations to deliver education programs to producers; establishment of producer associations or cooperatives as a point of contact between governments and individual producers; microcredit financing to support cooperative value-added and environmentally appropriate production and processing technologies; and development of codes of good practice and related education programs for sustainable, environmentally appropriate production.

Enforcement through civil society, external stakeholders, and informational campaigns

Civil society and, increasingly, external stakeholders have always played a significant role in advocating for social and environmental standards and monitoring their implementation—in particular, where institutions are weak. Civil society organizations are particularly useful in solving problems of collective action, which can arise when damages hurt many households, but organizing to present their case is difficult. Civil society organizations can be local (representing the interests of natives), but also international (i.e., representing the interests of consumers who care about buying products produced under strong social and environmental safeguards or who have an interest in the environment as a

global public good). The growing interest of foreign consumers in buying socially and environmentally friendly products has opened new markets and provided incentives for firms to subscribe to verifiable product certification programs (organic, fair trade, environmental sustainability, etc.) to maintain or improve market share.

Another additional policy measure that is not normally considered environmental but that can reduce environmental damage is institutional freedom of information laws and other legal means to empower civil society to assist in enforcing national regulations and standards and holding government and industry accountable. Management instruments based on information disclosure include labeling, rating, and certification. "Organic" is a common label for food and is one of the oldest schemes, whereas "shade-grown coffee" is a new and successful one. The "dolphin safe" label, granted by the Earth Island Institute, has had a tremendous impact on tuna fishing practices.

Fisheries management

Management of common-property resources such as fisheries may combine voluntary cooperation among exploiters of the resource, government management, and influence of civil society. LAC has several examples that could serve as models. In Honduras and Nicaragua, producers and buyers are collaborating to develop sustainable value chains for the Caribbean spiny lobster. Meanwhile, the United States—the main market for the product—has passed legislation on the minimum size for imported lobsters to complement the local regulations. Similar alliances are emerging as farmers in Costa Rica export fresh farmed tilapia to U.S. markets. Learning from past fisheries collapses, scallop fishers in the San Matias Gulf in Argentina and "loco" fishers in Chile have formed self-regulating groups. In Mexico, the Baja California lobster cooperatives have achieved Marine Stewardship Council certification for sustainable seafood production, the gold standard for small-scale producers. Founded on sound science and with World Bank assistance, a vessel quota system was recently established in Peru. It is generating increasing economic returns in the anchoveta fishery and is engaging in the Marine Stewardship Council process for certification.

Reducing negative social impacts of extractive industries

One of the most important steps to avoid or minimize social impacts and conflict associated with extractive industries must be taken well in advance of the project itself: invest in the titling of lands in areas identified for future projects and assess any existing juridical conflicts regarding land tenure.

Second, to avoid misunderstandings and unrealistic expectations, before any contact between the company and the local people, the government should establish a formal process to educate local residents on the basic economics of the project (including a realistic estimate of its job intake capacity) and its potential for benefiting the community through compensation, the creation of local services, and the distribution of royalties from the project. Experience shows that the flow of information should start as early as possible so that people can think about the issues, consider the implications, formulate their views, and participate actively in the licensing process.

Third, to strengthen local capacity to negotiate, the government, in partnership with the project operators, should assess the needs for capacity building and develop a series of process-supporting training activities for local stakeholders, including the local government. In Peru, for example, a component of the Peru-Canada Project will support capacity building for the Energy and Mines Ministry regional offices and will help to strengthen the ministry's presence in local communities. In the Amazon region, the Program Energia, Ambiente y Poblacion, a joint initiative by OLADE (the Latin American Energy Organization) and the World Bank, seeks to support governments, industry, and indigenous people in their dialogue for developing common criteria to improve the handling of environmental and social impacts of oil operations.

Fourth, transparency can go a long way toward reducing suspicions and the potential for conflict.

Audited public reports with performance indicators and information on compensation agreements can bring transparency by showing how companies are managing the environmental and social impacts of their projects.

Fifth, all possible steps should be taken to avoid resettlement. Even if carried out properly, resettlement causes grave disruption to people's lives and is a costly process requiring experienced institutions. When resettlement is unavoidable, displaced populations should be compensated at full replacement cost for losses of assets and assisted in restoring their community ties and capacity to earn a living. Especially where land is the only means of livelihood available to the local people, resettlement should follow the land-for-land principle.

And, where there are environmental legacies, governments should assess the possibility of launching a fund to support remediation and reach compensation agreements with the affected populations.

Endnotes

1. A similar point is made by Aizenman and Glick (2008), who show in a formal model that the optimal portfolio composition for a sovereign wealth fund focused on long-term goals will include more risky assets than will the portfolio of a central bank accumulating assets for the purpose of stabilization.

2. See www.ft.com/cms/s/0/6b961aa2-e42c-11de-bed0-00 144feab49a.html?SID=google.

3. Chile's total investment in R&D as a percentage of GDP was 0.68% in 2004, which is high in comparison with other countries in the region, such as Argentina (0.44%), Peru (0.16%), and Uruguay (0.26%), but lower than Brazil (0.83%) and developed countries such as the United States (2.72%) and Japan (3.07%).

4. This is described in Política Nacional de Innovación para la Competitividad: Orientaciones y Plan de Acción 2009-10. Ministerio de Economía.

5. Peru was admitted as a candidate country by the EITI Board in September 2007 and has until September 2010 to complete the validation process. A draft report has been produced (on revenues), and Ernst and Young have been selected to reconcile the first report.

Appendix

Hydrocarbon and Copper Revenue Stabilization Funds and Fiscal Rules in LAC

| | Fiscal arrangement | Fiscal rule | | | Natural resource fund | | |
| | | | | | | | |
Country	Name/date established	Numerical rule	Compliance	Objectives	Accumulation rules	Withdrawal rules	Investment policy
Chile	Fiscal rule, 2000, followed by Fiscal Responsibility Law (FRL), 2006.	Structural overall balance (adjusted for temporary fluctuations in the copper price and economic activity). No explicit numerical target in FRL 2006 for structural surplus/balance.	Structural surplus target decreased to 0.5% of GDP from its initial level of 1% in 2007 (taking effect from 2008). Further reduced to 0% in 2009.	Saving; stabilization	FRL 2006 sets out that any surpluses generated go into two investment funds: the FRP and FEES.		
	Pension Reserve Fund (FRP)			Saving	Fiscal surpluses first destined for FRP up to a maximum of 0.5% of GDP.	To be used to finance unfunded pension commitments from 2016 onwards.	Authorized to invest 100% abroad.
	Economic and social stabilization fund (FEES), 2006			Stabilization	All fiscal surpluses in excess of 1% of GDP to go into the fund.	During periods of adverse terms of trade shocks, the resources of the fund will be available to maintain fiscal spending.	Authorized to invest 100% abroad.
Ecuador	Savings and contingency fund (FAC), 2005–08.			Saving; stabilization	20% of revenue from heavy crude oil.	Resources may be used if (i) actual oil revenue is below budgeted level or (ii) a national emergency is declared.	Account at central bank. No explicit investment policy.
	Oil stabilization fund (FEP), 1999–2007			Stabilization	Light crude revenue in excess of budgeted amount.	Earmarked spending in the following years.	Account at central bank. No explicit investment policy.
	Special account for social and productive investment, scientific development and fiscal stabilization (CEREPS), 2005–08			Stabilization	State revenue from heavy crude oil production and 45% of oil revenues above those in the annual budget, and after earmarks for regional projects.	Low-interest credit lines, old debt to social security, debt buybacks, infrastructure projects, social investment, research and development, roads, environment, stabilization of oil revenues, and emergencies.	

	Energy and Hydrocarbon Investment Fund, 2006–08 (FEISEH)	Stabilization	All net oil revenues from the Bloque 15 field, formerly operated by Occidental Petroleum.	27% to CEREPS; reimbursement of Petroecuador costs for Bloque 15, US$145 million for the budget, electricity, hydrocarbon investments, and others	
	FRL, 2002, 2005 Abolished in 2008.	Expenditures; non-oil balance; debt	Fiscal outcomes were not consistent with the expenditure and deficit ceilings. Changes in the FRL (2005) loosened the rules.		
	Amazon Development Fund, 2000	Construction and maintenance of roads	Until 2005, 25% of the oil revenues for the Oil Stabilization Fund was channeled into the Amazon development fund, and after 2005, 50%.		
	Law of 2008	Current spending cannot be financed with revenues arising from public debt operations or oil exports.	Ecuador eliminated the oil funds and almost all other oil-revenue earmarks in April 2008. Only the earmarks for the Amazon Development Fund were maintained.		
Mexico	Oil stabilization fund, 2000	Saving; stabilization	PEMEX duty on hydrocarbons for the fund plus 40% (proportion has varied over time, it was temporarily increased to 65% for 2010) of oil revenue in excess of the revenue assumed in the budget, after first taking into account offsetting increases in nonprogrammable expenditures.	Discretionary transfers to the budget if oil revenues are below those projected in the budget. However, congress can deplete the fund by majority vote.	Deposits at central bank. Counterpart assets in foreign currency.

(continued)

Hydrocarbon and Copper Revenue Stabilization Funds and Fiscal Rules in LAC

	Fiscal arrangement		Fiscal rule		Natural resource fund			
Country	Name/date established		Numerical rule	Compliance	Objectives	Accumulation rules	Withdrawal rules	Investment policy
	Budget and Fiscal Responsibility Law, 2006		Target is a balanced budget fiscal rule (zero cash balance for the budgetary public sector); changes require justification and plans for returning to zero balance.	2008 PEMEX reform accompanied by modifications of the FRL. Starting with 2009 budget, the calculation of fiscal target excludes capital spending by PEMEX. This will create room for 0.6% of GDP in higher spending in 2009 (for infrastructure investment).	Stabilization	Revenue in excess of budgeted amounts first used to compensate for unforeseeable budget overruns. The remainder is split among four-tier funds—a stabilization fund, and funds to finance Pemex investment and investment by federal entities.	If total revenues are less than budgeted due to lower oil prices or exchange rate movements, transfers may be made from the oil stabilization funds to Pemex or the budget to cover the budget shortfall.	
Trinidad & Tobago	Interim revenue stabilization fund (IRSF), 2000, and later Heritage and stabilization fund, 2007				Stabilization; Savings	60% of oil and gas revenues in excess of budget amounts, usually based on an estimate of the long-term oil price.	Government can tap up to 60% oil and gas net revenue shortfalls, but not exceeding 25% of the fund, provided that the shortfall is at least 10% of budget revenues.	Deposits at central bank. Funds invested in foreign assets with a medium to long-term focus.

Sources: Ossowski, Villafuerte, Medas, and Thomas (2008); Davis, Ossowski, and Fedelino (2003), IMF (2010b); da Costa and Olivo (2008).

References

Acemoglu, Daron, Simon Johnson, and James A. Robinson. 2005. "The Rise of Europe: Atlantic Trade, Institutional Change and Economic Growth." *American Economic Review* 95(3): 546–79.

———. 2002. "Reversal of Fortune: Geography and Institutions in the Making of the Modern World Income Distribution." *Quarterly Journal of Economics* 117 (November): 1231–94.

———. 2001. "The Colonial Origins of Comparative Development: An Empirical Investigation." *American Economic Review* 91: 1369–401.

Acemoglu, Daron, and Fabrizio Zilibotti. 1997. "Was Prometheus Unbound by Chance? Risk, Diversification and Growth." *Journal of Political Economy* 105(4): 709–51.

Aizenman, J., and R. Glick. 2008. "Sovereign Wealth Funds: Stylized Facts about Their Determinants and Governance." Working Paper 14562 (December). National Bureau of Economic Research, Cambridge, MA.

Alderman, Harold, and Christina H. Paxson. 1992. "Do the Poor Insure? A Synthesis of the Literature on Risk and Consumption in Developing Countries." Policy Research Working Paper Series 1008. World Bank, Washington, DC.

Alesina, Alberto, Filipe R. Campante, and Guido Tabellini. 2008. "Why Is Fiscal Policy Often Procyclical?" *Journal of the European Economic Association* 6(5): 1006–36.

Alexeev, M., and R. Conrad. 2009. "The Elusive Curse of Oil." *The Review of Economics and Statistics* 91(3): 586–98.

Anaya, R. 2001. "Acute Elemental Mercury Poisoning in Three Locations of the Department of Cajamarca-Peru." *Toxicology* 164(1–3): 69.

Andres, A., J. L. Guasch, T. Haven, and V. Foster. 2008. "Participation in Infrastructure: Lights, Shadows, and the Road Ahead." Report 45625. Public Private Partnership Advisory Facility and the World Bank, Washington, DC.

Aragon, Fernando M., and Juan Pablo Rud. 2009. "The Blessing of Natural Resources: Evidence from a Peruvian Gold Mine." Banco Central de Peru, Lima. Working Paper Series DT, 2009-015 (December).

Auty, Richard. 1993. *Sustaining Development in Mineral Economies: The Resource Curse Thesis.* New York: Taylor and Francis.

Balagtas, Joseph V., and Matthew T. Holt. 2009. "The Commodity Terms of Trade, Unit Roots, and Nonlinear Alternatives: A Smooth Transition Approach." *American Journal of Agricultural Economics* 91(1): 87–105.

Baland, Jean-Marie, and Patrick Francois. 2000. "Rent-Seeking and Resource Booms." *Journal of Development Economics* 61(2): 527–42.

Baxter, Marianne, and Michael A. Kouparitsas. 2006. "What Can Account for Fluctuations in the Terms of Trade?" *International Finance* 9(1): 63–86.

Becker, G. S., and I. Ehrlich. 1972. "Market Insurance, Self-insurance, and Self Protection." *Journal of Political Economy* 80(4): 623–48.

Blomstrom, M., and P. Meller. 1991. "Issues for Development: Lessons from Scandinavia and Latin American Development." In *Diverging Paths: Comparing a Century of Scandinavian and Latin American Development*, ed. M. Blomstrom and P. Meller. Washington, DC: Inter-American Development Bank.

Bornhorst, Fabian, Sanjeev Gupta, and John Thornton. 2009. "Natural Resource Endowments and the Domestic Revenue Effort." *European Journal of Political Economy* 25(4): 439–46.

Borum, Michael. 2009. "Rio Blanco: Massive Copper Project Proposed for Cloud Forest." Oxfam America. March 3, http://www.oxfamamerica.org/articles/rio-blanco-massive-copper-project-proposed-for-cloud-forest.

Brambilla, Irene, Rafael Dix Carneiro, Daniel Lederman, and Guido Porto. 2010. "Skills, Exports, and the Wages of Five Million Latin American Workers," Policy Research Working Paper 5246 World Bank, Washington, DC.

Brambilla, Irene, and Guido Porto. 2009. "Household Dependence on Commodities in Latin American and the Caribbean." Background paper for this report.

Brollo, F., T. Nannicini, R. Perotti, and G. Tabellini. 2010. "The Political Resource Curse." Working Paper 15705. National Bureau of Economic Research, Cambridge, MA.

Brunnschweiler, Christa N. 2008. "Cursing the Blessings? Natural Resource Abundance, Institutions, and Economic Growth." *World Development* 36(3): 399–419.

Brunnschweiler, Christa N., and Erwin H. Bulte. 2008. "Linking Natural Resources to Slow Growth and More Conflict." *Science* 320 (May): 616–17.

Brunnschweiler, Christa N., and Erwin H. Bulte. 2008. "The Resource Curse Revisited and Revised: A Tale of Paradoxes and Red Herrings." *Journal of Environmental Economics and Management* 55(3): 248–64.

Buchanan, J. M., and G. Tullock. 1962. *The Calculus of Consent, Logical Foundations of Constitutional Democracy.* Ann Arbor: University of Michigan Press.

Byrne, Joseph, Giorgio Fazio, and Norbert Fiess. 2010. "Panel Data Study of Common Factors in a Commodity Price Index." Background paper for this report.

Cairnes, J. E. 1873. *Essays in Political Economy.* London: Macmillan.

Calderon, C., and P. Fajnzylber. 2009. "How Much Room Does Latin America and the Caribbean Have for Implementing Counter-cyclical Fiscal Policies?" Latin America and Caribbean Crisis Briefs Series. World Bank, Washington, DC.

Camacho, Máximo, and Gabriel Pérez. 2010. "Commodity Prices and the Business Cycle in Latin America: Living and Dying by Commodities?" Background paper for this report.

Caselli, F., and G. Michaels. 2009. "Do Oil Windfalls Improve Living Standards? Evidence from Brazil." Working Paper 15550. National Bureau of Economic Research, Cambridge, MA.

Cashin, Paul Anthony, and C. John McDermott. 2002. "The Long-Run Behavior of Commodity Prices: Small Trends and Big Variability." Working Paper. International Monetary Fund, Washington, DC.

CATAPA. 2009. "Peru: The Majaz Case." Available at http://www.catapa.be/en/south-action/peru.

Chang, Roberto, Constantino Hevia, and Norman Loayza. 2009. "Privatization and Nationalization Cycles." Policy Research Working Paper 5029. World Bank, Washington, DC.

Chong, Alberto, and Florencio Lopez de Silanes, eds.. 2005 *Privatization in Latin America: Myths and Reality.* Stanford, CA: Stanford University Press and the World Bank, February.

Chua, Amy L. 1995. "The Privatization-Nationalization Cycle: The Link between Markets and Ethnicity in Developing Countries." *Columbia Law Review* 95(2): 223–303.

Coelli, Tim J., and D. S. Prasada Rao. 2005. "Total Factor Productivity Growth in Agriculture: A Malmquist Index Analysis of 93 Countries, 1980–2000." *International Association of Agricultural Economists* 32(s1): 115–34.

Collier, Paul, and Benedikt Goderis. 2007. "Commodity Prices, Growth and the Natural Resources Curse: Reconciling a Conundrum." Working Paper 276 (August). Centre for the Study of African Economies, Oxford.

Corden, W. M. 1984. "Booming Sector and Dutch Disease Economics: Survey and Consolidation." *Oxford Economic Papers* 36: 359–80.

Corden, W. M., and J. P. Neary. 1983. "Booming Sector and De-industrialisation in a Small Open Economy." *Economic Journal* 92: 825–48.

Cuddington, John. 1989. "Commodity Export Booms in Developing Countries." *World Bank Research Observer* 4: 143–65.

Cuddington, John, and D. Jerrett. 2008. "SuperCycles in Real Metals Prices?" *IMF Staff Papers* 55(4): 541–65.

Cuddington, John, Rodney Ludema, and Shamila Jayasuriya. 2007. "Prebisch-Singer Redux." In *Natural Resources and Development: Are They a Curse? Are They Destiny?*, ed. Daniel Lederman and William F. Maloney. Washington, DC: World Bank/Stanford University Press.

Cunha, Barbara, Carlos Prada, and Emily Sinnott. 2009a. "A Contemporaneous Commodity Export Price Index for Latin American and Caribbean Countries." Background paper for this report.

———. 2009b. "Duration Analysis for Commodity Booms/Slumps in Latin American and the Caribbean." Background paper for this report.

Das, U. S., Y. Lu, C. Muldser, and A. Sy. 2009. "Setting Up a Sovereign Wealth Fund: Some Policy and Operational Considerations." Working Paper WP/09/179 (August). International Monetary Fund, Washington, DC.

David, Paul A., and Gavin Wright. 1997. "Increasing Returns and the Genesis of American Resource Abundance." *Industrial and Corporate Change* 6(2): 203–45.

———. 1995. "The Origins of American Resource Abundance." Research Memoranda 017. Maastricht Economic Research Institute on Innovation and Technology, Maastricht.

Davis, J. M., R. Ossowski, and A. Fedelino. 2003. *Fiscal Policy Formulation and Implementation in Oil-Producing Economies.* Washington, DC: International Monetary Fund.

Deaton, Angus. 1999. "Commodity Prices and Growth in Africa." *Journal of Economic Perspectives* 13(3): 23–40.

———. 1991. "Savings and Liquidity Constraints." *Econometrica* 59(5): 1221–48.

De Ferranti, D., G. E. Perry, D. Lederman, and W. F. Maloney. 2002. *From Natural Resources to the Knowledge Economy: Trade and Job Quality.* Latin American and Caribbean Studies. World Bank, Washington, DC.

Dercon, S. 2004. "Risk, Insurance and Poverty." In *Insurance against Poverty*, ed. S. Dercon. Oxford: Oxford University Press.

Díaz-Cayeros, Alberto. 2009. "Political Economy Analysis of Averting the Resource Curse: Mexico Case Study." Background paper for this report.

Di Giovanni, Julian, and Andrei A. Levchenko. 2009. "Firm Entry, Trade, and Welfare in Zipf's World.". Research Seminar in International Economics Working Paper 591. University of Michigan, Ann Arbor.

Drazen, Allan. 2000. *Political Economy in Macroeconomics.* Princeton, NJ: Princeton University Press.

Duncan, Roderick. 2006. "Price or Politics? An Investigation of the Causes of Expropriation." *Australian Journal of Agricultural and Resource Economics* 50(1): 85–101.

Dunning, Thad. 2009. "The Political Economy of the Resource Paradox." Background paper for this report.

———. 2008. *Crude Democracy: Natural Resource Wealth and Political Regimes.* Cambridge Studies in Comparative Politics. New York: Cambridge University Press.

Easterly, William, and Aart Kraay. 2000. "Small States, Small Problems? Income, Growth and Volatility in Small States." *World Development* 28: 2013–27.

Eastwood, R. K., and A. J. Venables. 1982. "The Macroeconomic Implications of a Resource Discovery in an Open Economy." *Economic Journal, Royal Economic Society* 92(366): 285–99.

Enders, K., and H. Herberg. 1983. "The Dutch Disease: Causes, Consequences, Cures and Calamities." *Weltwinschaftliches Archiv* 119 (3).

Engel, Eduardo, Christopher Nielsen, and Rodrigo Valdés. 2010. "Fiscal Rules as Social Policy." Background paper for this report.

Engerman, Stanley L., and Kenneth L. Sokoloff. 2003. "Institutional and Non-Institutional Explanations of Economic Differences." Working Paper w9989 (September). National Bureau of Economic Research, Cambridge, MA.

———. 1997. "Factor Endowments, Institutions, and Differential Paths of Growth among New World Economies: A View from Economic Historians of the United States." In *How Latin America Fell Behind,* ed. S. Haber. Stanford, CA: Stanford University Press.

Fafchamps, Marcel, Christopher Udry, and Katherine Czukas. 1998. "Drought and Saving in West Africa: Are livestock a Buffer Stock?" *Journal of Development Economics* 55(2): 273–305.

Fatás, Antonio. 2002. "The Effects of Business Cycles on Growth." Working Paper 156. Central Bank of Chile, Santiago.

Fatás, Antonio, and Ilian Mihov. 2003. "The Case for Restricting Fiscal Policy Discretion." *Quarterly Journal of Economics* 118(4): 1419–47.

Frankel, Jeffrey A. 2009. "A Comparison of Monetary Anchor Options for Commodity-Exporters in Latin America and the Caribbean." Background paper for this report.

———. 2003. "A Proposed Monetary Regime for Small Commodity Exporters: Peg the Export Price (PEP)." *International Finance* 6(1): 61–88.

Frankel, Jeffrey A., and Ayako Saiki. 2002. "A Proposal to Anchor Monetary Policy by the Price of the Export Commodity," *Journal of Economic Integration* 17(3): 417–48.

Gavin, M., and R. Perotti. 1997. "Fiscal Policy in Latin America." In *NBER Macroeconomics Annual 1997*, ed. B. Bernanke and J. Rotemberg. Cambridge, MA: MIT Press.

Gelb, A. 1990. *Oil Windfalls: Blessing or Curse? A Comparative Study of Six Developing Exporters.* Oxford: Oxford University Press.

Gregory, R. G. 1976. "Some Implications of the Growth of the Mineral Sector." *Australian Journal of Agricultural Economics* 20(2): 71–91.

Grilli, Enzo, and Maw Cheng Yang. 1988. "Primary Commodity Prices, Manufactured Goods Prices, and the Terms of Trade of Developing Countries: What the Long Run Shows." *World Bank Economic Review* 2(1): 1–47.

Grubel, H. G. and P. J. Lloyd. 1975. *Intra-Industry Trade: The Theory and Measurement of International Trade in Differentiated Products.* New York: Wiley.

Guriev, Sergei, Antón Kolotilin, and Konstantin Sonin. 2008. "Determinants of Expropriation in the Oil Sector: A Theory and Evidence from Panel Data." Discussion Paper 6755. Centre for Economic Policy Research, London.

Haber, Stephen, and Victor Menaldo. 2009. "Do Natural Resources Fuel Authoritarianism? A Reappraisal of the Resource Curse." Working paper, Department of Political Science, Stanford University.

Hausmann, R., and M. Gavin. 1996. "Securing Stability and Growth in a Shock Prone Region: The Policy Challenge for Latin America." Working Paper 315. Inter-American Development Bank, Office of the Chief Economist, Washington, DC.

Hausmann, R., J. Hwang, and D. Rodrik. 2005. "What You Export Matters." Working Paper 11905. National Bureau of Economic Research, Cambridge, MA. http://www.nber.org/papers/w11905.

Heckscher, E. F. 1919/1991. "The Effect of Foreign Trade on the Distribution of Income." In Heckscher-Ohlin Trade Theory, ed./trans. H. Flam and M. J. Flanders. Cambridge, MA: MIT Press.

Hnatkovska, V., and N., Loayza. 2005. "Volatility and Growth." Working Paper 3184. World Bank, Washington, DC.

IFC (International Finance Corporation). 2002. "Global Mining, an Asset for Competitiveness: Sound Environmental Management in Mining Countries." Mining and Development Series, no. 26853. IFC, Washington, DC

IMF (International Monetary Fund). 2010a. "Mexico: 2010 Article IV Consultation." Staff Report (March), IMF Country Report 10/71. IMF, Washington, DC.

———. 2010b. "Mexico: Chapter III." Selected Issues Paper (March), IMF Country Report 10/70. IMF, Washington, DC.

———. 2009a. Regional Economic Outlook: Western Hemisphere Crisis Averted—What's Next? Washington, DC: IMF.

———. 2009b. "Chile: 2009 Article IV Consultation." Staff Report (September), IMF Country Report 09/271. IMF, Washington, DC.

———. 2009c. "Fiscal Rules—Anchoring Expectations for Sustainable Public Finances." Prepared by the Fiscal Affairs Department. (In consultation with other departments), December 16, 2009.

Isham, J., L. Pritchett, M. Woolcock, and G. Busby. 2003. "The Varieties of Resource Experience: How Natural Resource Export Structures Affect the Political Economy of Economic Growth." World Bank Economic Review 19(1): 141–64.

Jalan, J., and M. Ravallion. 1999. "Are the Poor Less Well-Insured? Evidence on Vulnerability to Income Risk in Rural China." Journal of Development Economics 58: 61–81

Jansen, M. 2004. "Income Volatility in Small and Developing Economies: Export Concentration Matters." WTO Discussion Paper no. 3. World Trade Organization, Geneva.

Janssens, Daan. 2009. "Mining Conflict in Peru Leaves Two Dead." CATAPA. April 12. http://www.catapa.be/en/news/614.

Johnson-Calari, Jennifer, and Malan Rietveld, eds. 2007. Sovereign Wealth Management. London: Central Banking Publications.

Karl, Terry Lynn. 1997. The Paradox of Plenty: Oil Booms and Petro-States. Berkeley: University of California Press.

Keynes, J. M. 1942/1974. "The International Control of Raw Materials." Journal of International Economics 4: 299–315.

Kiguel, Miguel, and M. Okseniuk 2010. "Commodity Prices and Exchange Rate Policies during the Recent Boom and Bust in LAC." Background paper for this report.

Knack, Stephen. 2008. "Sovereign Rents and the Quality of Tax Policy and Administration." World Bank Policy Research Working Paper WPS 4773. World Bank, Washington, DC.

Knudsen, Odin, and Andrew Parnes. 1975. Trade Instability and Economic Development: An Empirical Study. Lexington, MA: Lexington Books.

Kobrin, Stephen J. 1984. "Expropriation as an Attempt to Control Foreign Firms in LDCs: Trends from 1960 to 1979." International Studies Quarterly 28(3): 329–48.

Kolstad, Ivar, and Arne Wiig. 2009. "It's the Rents, Stupid! The Political Economy of the Resource Curse." Energy Policy 37(12): 5317–325.

Lane, Philip R., and Aaron Tornell. 1996. "Power, Growth, and the Voracity Effect." Journal of Economic Growth 1(2): 213–41.

La Porta, Rafael, and Florencio Lopez de Silanes. 1999. "The Benefits of Privatization: Evidence from Mexico." Quarterly Journal of Economics 114(4): 1193–242.

Leamer, Edward. 1984. Sources of International Comparative Advantage: Theory and Evidence. Cambridge, MA: MIT Press.

Lederman, David, and William F. Maloney. Forthcoming, Trade Quality: Does What You Export Matter? Washington, DC: World Bank, Latin America and Caribbean Region.

———. 2008. "In Search of the Missing Resource Curse." Economía 9(1): 1–58.

———. 2006. "Trade Structure and Growth." In Natural Resources: Neither Curse nor Destiny, ed. D. Lederman and W. F. Maloney, 15–39. Palo Alto, CA: Stanford University Press.

———, eds. 2006. Natural Resources: Neither Curse nor Destiny. Palo Alto, CA: Stanford University Press.

Lederman, Daniel, and Colin Xu. "Commodity Dependence and Macroeconomic Volatility: The Structural versus the Macroeconomic Management Hypothesis." Background paper for this report.

Loayza, Norman V., Romain Rancière, Luis Servén, and Jaume Ventura. 2007. "Macroeconomic Volatility and Welfare in Developing Countries: An Introduction." World Bank Economic Review 21(3): 343–57.

London Mining Network. 2009. "News about Monterrico Metals' Rio Blanco Project." March 31. http://londonminingnetwork.org/2009/04/news-about-monterrico-metals-rio-blanco-project-peru/.

Lopez, Humberto. 2008. "The Social Discount Rate: Estimates for Nine Latin American Countries." Policy Research Working Paper 4639. World Bank, Washington, DC.

Mahdavy, Hussein. 1970. "The Patterns and Problems of Economic Development in Rentier States: The Case of Iran." In Studies in Economic History of the Middle East, ed. M. A. Cook. London: Oxford University Press.

Maloney, W. F. 2007. "Missed Opportunities: Innovation and Resource Based Growth in Latin America." In Natural Resources: Neither Curse nor Destiny, ed. D. Lederman and W. F. Maloney, 15–39. Palo Alto, CA: Stanford University Press.

Mandel, B. 2009. "The Differentiation and Dynamics of Latin American Commodity Exports." Background paper for this report.

Manzano, Osmel, and Francisco Monaldi. 2008. "The Political Economy of Oil Production in Latin America." *Economía* 9(1): 99–103.

Martin, W., and D. Mitra. 2001. "Productivity Growth and Convergence in Agriculture versus Manufacturing." *Economic Development and Cultural Change* 49(2): 403–22.

Medas, Paulo, and Daria Zakharova. 2008. "A Primer on Fiscal Analysis in Oil-Producing Countries." Working Paper WP/09/56. International Monetary Fund, Washington, DC.

Mehlum, H., K. Moene, and R. Torvik. 2006. "Institutions and the Resource Curse." *Economic Journal* 116: 1–20.

Minor, Michael S. 1994. "The Demise of Expropriation as an Instrument of LDC Policy, 1980–1992." *Journal of International Business Studies* 25(1): 177–88.

MMSCD (Mining, Minerals and Sustainable Development). 2002. *Breaking New Ground: The Report of the MMSCD Project.* London: Earthscan.

Naim, Moises. 2009. "Oil Can Be a Curse on Poor Nations." *Financial Times.* August 18. FT.Com. www.ft.com/cms/s/0/abda323c-8c21-11de-b14f-00144feabdc0.html?catid=9&SID=google.

Napoli, Enzo, and Patricio Navia. 2010. "Government Policies and the Evolution of Copper Mining in Chile, 1973–2008." Background paper for this report.

Nash, J. 1990. "Export Instability and Long-Term Capital Flows: Response to Asset Risk in a Small Economy." *Economic Inquiry* 28 (April): 307–16.

Newbery, D. M. G., and J. E. Stiglitz. 1981. *The Theory of Price Stabilization: A Study in the Economics of Risk.* Oxford: Clarendon Press.

North, Douglass C. 1990. *Institutions, Institutional Change and Economic Performance.* Cambridge: Cambridge University Press.

North, Douglass C., John Joseph Wallis, Steven B. Webb, and Barry R. Weingast. 2007. "Limited Access Orders in the Developing World: A New Approach to the Problems of Development." Policy Research Working Paper 4359, September. World Bank, Washington, DC.

Nyamukure, B. 2008. "Contextualizing Payment for Environmental Services Potential in Mzingwane, Zimbabwe." Center for Applied Social Sciences, University of Zimbabwe, Zimbabwe.

OLADE (Latin America Energy Organization). 2007. *Targeting Fuel Subsidies in Latin America and the Caribbean: Analysis and Proposal.* Quito: OLADE Technical Articles.

Olivo, Victor, and Mercedes da Costa. 2008. "Constraints on the Design and Implementation of Monetary Policy in Oil Economies: The Case of Venezuela." Working Paper 8(142). International Monetary Fund, Washington, DC.

Organization of American States. 2010. Database of Projects of Payments for Ecosystem Services in Latin America and the Caribbean. http://www.apps.oas.org/pes/default.aspx.

O'Ryan, R., M. Nitlitschek, E. Niklitschek, A. Ulloa, and N. Gligo. 2010. "Trade Liberalization, Rural Poverty, and the Environment: A Case Study of the Forest and Salmon Sectors in Chile." In *Vulnerable Places, Vulnerable People: Trade Liberalization, Rural Poverty, and the Environment,* ed. J. Cook, O. Cylke, D. Larson, J. Nash, and P. Stedman-Edwards. Northampton, MA: Elgar.

Ossowski, R., M. Villafuerte, P. A. Medas, and T. Thomas. 2008. *Managing the Oil Revenue Boom: The Role of Fiscal Institutions.* Washington, DC: International Monetary Fund.

Pagiola, S. 2006. *Payment for Environmental Services: An Introduction.* Washington, DC: World Bank.

Perry, Guillermo, and Mauricio Olivera. 2009. "Natural Resources, Institutions and Economic Performance." Working Paper, November 15. Fundación para la Educación Superior y el Desarrollo (Fedesarrollo), Bogota.

Peruanista. 2009. "News about Monterrico Metals Mining Company and the Rio Blanco Project." October 20. http://peruanista.blogspot.com/2009/10/british-company-supported-by-perus.html.

Pfaffenzeller, Stephan, Paul Newbold, and Anthony Rayner. 2007. "A Short Note on Updating the Grilli and Yang Commodity Price Index." *World Bank Economic Review* 21: 1–47.

Prebisch, R. 1949. O desenvolvimento economico da America Latina e seus principais problemas [The Economic Development of Latin America and Its Principal Problems]. *Revista Brasileira de Economia* 3: 47–100.

Ram, Justin, and Giovanni Ruta. 2009. "Natural Resource Depletion and Sustainability in Latin America and the Caribbean." Background paper for this report.

Ramey, Garey, and Valerie A. Ramey. 1995. "Cross-Country Evidence on the Link between Volatility and Growth." *American Economic Review* 85(5): 1138–51.

Regunaga, Marcelo. 2010. "The Soybean Chain in Argentina." Background paper for this report.

Rodrik, D. 2004 . "Industrial Policy for the Twenty-first Century." John F. Kennedy School of Government Working Paper. http://ideas.repec .org/p/cpr/ceprdp/4767.html.

———. 1997. "Trade, Social Insurance, and the Limits to Globalization." Working Paper 5905. National Bureau of Economic Research, Cambridge, MA.

Rosenzweig, Mark R., and Hans P. Binswanger. 1993. "Wealth, Weather Risk and the Profitability of Agricultural Investment." *Economic Journal* 103 (January): 56–78.

Rosenzweig, Mark R., and Kenneth I. Wolpin. 1993. "Credit Market Constraints, Consumption Smoothing and the Accumulation of Durable Production Assets in Low-Income

Countries: Investments in Bullocks in India." *Journal of Political Economy* 101(2).

Ross, Michael L. 2010. "Oil and Democracy Revisited." Manuscript. Department of Political Science, University of California, Los Angeles. http://www.sscnet.ucla.edu/polisci/faculty/ross/.

————. 2001. "Does Oil Hinder Democracy?" *World Politics* 53(3): 325–61.

Sachs, J. D., and A. Warner. 1997. *Natural Resource Abundance and Economic Growth.* Cambridge, MA: Center for International Development and Harvard Institute for International Development.

————. 1995. "Economic Reform and the Process of Global Integration." *Brookings Papers on Economic Activity* 1: 1–95.

Sala-i-Martin, Xavier, Gernot Doppelhofer, and Ronald I. Miller. 2004. "Determinants of Long-Term Growth: A Bayesian Averaging of Classical Estimates (BACE) Approach." *American Economic Review* 94(4): 813–35.

Salazar, Milagros. 2007. "Mining Project Hurting Highland Ecosystem." IPS News. September 12. http://ipsnews.net/news.asp?idnews=39233.

Schmitz, James A., Jr., and Arilton Teixeira. 2008. "Privatizations Impact on Private Productivity: The Case of Brazilian Iron Ore." *Review of Economic Dynamics* 11(4): 745–60.

Shafik, Nemat. 1996. "Selling Privatization Politically." *Columbia Journal of World Business* 31(4): 20–29.

SIISE-STFS, Rob Vos, Juan Ponce, Mauricio León, José Cuestas, and Wladimir Brovorich. 2003. "El subsidio al gas y el Bono Solidario en el Ecuador." *Cuaderno* N.6. Quito.

Soifer, Hillel. 2006. "Authority over Distance: Explaining Variation in State Infrastructural Power in Latin America." Ph.D. dissertation. Department of Government, Harvard University.

Spraos, J. 1980. "The Statistical Debate on the Net Barter Terms of Trade between Primary Products and Manufactures." *Economic Journal* 90(357): 107–28.

Stijns, J. P. C. 2005. "Natural Resource Abundance and Economic Growth Revisited." *Resources Policy* 30(2): 107–30.

Talvi, E., and C. Vegh. 2005. "Tax Base Variability and Procyclicality of Fiscal Policy." *Journal of Development Economics* 78(1): 156–90.

Tornell, Aaron, and Philip R. Lane. 1999. "The Voracity Effect." *American Economic Review* 89(1): 22–46.

Torvik, R. 2002. "Natural Resources, Rent Seeking and Welfare." *Journal of Development Economics* 76: 455–70.

Valdés, A., and W. Foster. 2003. "The Positive Externalities of Chilean Agriculture: The Significance of Its Growth and Export Orientation, A Synthesis of the Roles of Agriculture Chile Case Study." December 18. Food and Agriculture Organization of the United Nations, Rome.

Van der Ploeg, F., and S. Poelheke. 2009. "Volatility and the Natural Resource Curse." *Oxford Economic Papers* 61: 727–60.

Vardy, Felix. 2010. "The Increasing Marginal Returns of Better Institutions." Background paper for this report.

Vasquez, Patricia. 2010. "In the Field: Peru." March 12. United States Institute for Peace, Washington, DC. http://www.usip.org/in-the-field/in-the-field-peru.

View from Peru. 2010. "Near Arequipa: Police/Miners Clash Leaves 6 Dead." April 6. http://birksnboots.blogspot.com/2010/04/near-arequipa-policeminers-clash-leaves.html.

Viner, J. 1952. *International Trade and Economic Development.* Oxford: Clarendon Press.

Waugh, F. V. 1944. "Does the Consumer Benefit from Instability?" *Quarterly Journal of Economics* 58: 602–14.

Webb, Steven. 2010. "Managing Mineral Wealth in Middle-Income Countries: Political Economy in Five Examples from Latin America." World Bank, unpublished manuscript.

Wicksell, K. 1916/1958. "The 'Critical Point' in the Law of Decreasing Agricultural Productivity." In *Selected Papers on Economic Theory*, ed. E. Lindahl. London: Allen and Unwin.

World Bank. 2010. "Chile: Review of Public Technological Institutes in the Agriculture Sector." Sustainable Development Department of the Latin America and Caribbean Region, Agriculture and Rural Development Cluster, Washington, DC.

————. 2009. *Global Economic Prospects: Commodities at the Crossroads.* Washington, DC: World Bank.

————. 2006. *Where Is the Wealth of Nations?* Washington, DC: World Bank.

————. 2005. "Wealth and Sustainability: The Environmental and Social Dimensions of the Mining Sector in Peru." Report 38044-PE (May). World Bank, Washington, DC.

World Bank–IADB. 2004. *Ecuador: Creating Fiscal Space for Poverty Reduction. A Fiscal Management and Public Expenditure Review.* Washington, DC: World Bank.

Wright, Gavin. 2001. "Resource-Based Growth Then and Now." Stanford University, prepared for the World Bank Project "Patterns of Integration in the Global Economy."

————. 2006. "Resource-Based Growth Past and Present." In *Natural Resources: Neither Curse nor Destiny*, ed. D. Lederman and W. F. Maloney. Palo Alto, CA: Stanford University Press.

————. 1990. "The Origins of American Industrial Success, 1879–1940." *American Economic Review* 80(4): 651–68.

Wright, Gavin, and Jesse Czelusta. 2004. "Why Economies Slow: The Myth of the Resource Curse." *Challenge* 47(2): 6–38.

WWF (World Wildlife Fund). 2010. "Payment for Environmental Services." http://peru.panda.org/en/our_work/in_peru/climate/services/.

ECO-AUDIT
Environmental Benefits Statement

The World Bank is committed to preserving endangered forests and natural resources. The Office of the Publisher follows the recommended standards for paper usage set by the Green Press Initiative, a nonprofit program supporting publishers in using fiber that is not from endangered forests.

In the printing of *Natural Resources in Latin America and the Caribbean,* we took the following measures to reduce our carbon footprint:

- We used paper containing 50 percent recycled fiber made from postconsumer waste; each pound of postconsumer recycled fiber that replaces a ton of virgin fiber prevents the release of 2,108 lbs. of greenhouse gas emissions and lessens the burden on landfills.
- We used paper that is chlorine-free and acid-free.

For more information, visit www.greenpress initiative.org.

Saved:
- 5 trees
- 1 million BTUs of total energy
- 430 lbs. of CO_2 equivalent of greenhouse gases
- 2,073 gallons of wastewater
- 126 lbs. of solid waste